A *Heartfelt*
Mission

A *Heartfelt* Mission

The West End Home Foundation
1891–2016

Mary Ellen Pethel

ORANGE *frazer* PRESS
Wilmington, Ohio

Published for Mary Ellen Pethel and
West End Home Foundation by:
Orange Frazer Press
P.O. Box 214
Wilmington, OH 45177
Telephone: 937.382.3196 for price and shipping information.
Website: www.orangefrazer.com

Book and cover design: Alyson Rua and Orange Frazer Press

Library of Congress Control Number: 2017949667

First Printing

From the Old Woman's Home to the West End Home for Ladies to the West End Home Foundation, more than two thousand women—including residents, Board members, Auxiliary members and employees—have contributed to the organization's financial and institutional success. This book is dedicated to their commitment, compassion and tireless support of our mission.

We would also like to extend a special thanks to Jean Dobson Farris and Gray Oliver Thornburg who recognized the importance of a written narrative to preserve the rich history of such a noble organization.

Jean Dobson Farris and Gray Oliver Thornburg

Acknowledgments

*I*n May 2013, I was honored to give the keynote address at the Step Singing ceremony at Harpeth Hall School as a part of the weekend's commencement events. "Write It Down" was the title, and the central theme of my remarks emphasized the importance of documenting legacy and memory in a digital age. Gray Thornburg was in the audience that evening as she celebrated her daughter's graduation. A week later, Gray reached out to me and scheduled a meeting. In early June, I met with three members of the WEHF Board of Directors: Gray Thornburg, Barbara Cannon, and Jean Farris. Lillian Harley, the last resident of the West End Home Foundation had recently passed away, and her death signaled the end of a momentous chapter for the organization. As the foundation transitioned to grantmaking fulltime, there was a pressing need and desire to preserve the West End Home Foundation's past for future generations with a written narrative that recorded and recognized the organization's rich history. I spent the summer researching their archival collection and was overcome with a sense of admiration and gratitude for the lives, work, and service of all those involved since the late 1880s. I quickly realized that this was a story that needed to be told and shared.

As the West End Home Foundation commemorates its 125th anniversary, this book affirms the history and mission of a nonprofit organization dedicated to improving the lives and care of seniors in Nashville and throughout Middle Tennessee. While we celebrate the past, it is the present-day support I have received that made this project possible. I would like to offer my deepest appreciation to members of the Board of Directors, book committee, and communications committee. Many thanks to Cammie Rash who chaired the book committee and helped to find and secure Orange Frazer Press for its publication. I would also like to thank Kim Hardin for writing the foreword and ably leading the WEHF as the current Board President.

In order to capture the last fifty years of the organization's history, I was fortunate enough to interview several individuals who gave willingly and graciously of their time. These individuals include: Cindy Dickinson, Jean Farris, Jay Grannis, Patricia Ingram Hart, Terronda Henderson, N. Courtney Hollins, Sarah McConnell, Peggy Miller, Carol Nelson, Jean Oldfield, Dianne Oliver, Gray Thornburg, and Gayle Vance. Their insight and institutional memory helped to inform much of the book's content. Jean Oldfield and Jean Farris deserve a special thank you as they helped to clarify names, dates, and the accuracy of the text on multiple occasions. I also consulted Ridley Wills II, historian and Nashville expert, who provided context and relevant information related to the Old Woman's Home and early Nashville history.

This project would not have been possible without Cindy Dickinson and Dianne Oliver. Cindy's herculean efforts in organizing, cataloging, and scanning thousands of pages led to the establishment of the *West End Home Foundation Collection* housed at the Metropolitan Archives. This collection, and her work, provided me with the necessary resources for this book. Dianne, WEHF Executive Director, answered countless calls and emails and helped to corral many moving parts. Both were invaluable throughout the process, and I thank them for their collaboration, time, attentiveness, and devotion to this project from beginning to end. The West End Home Foundation's future is bright in their very capable hands, and I am eternally grateful.

I also remain indebted to family and friends—to whom I owe a debt of gratitude. They have offered both support and patience over the last two years as I managed multiple writing projects and teaching loads. In addition, my editor, Judith Pierson, was instrumental throughout the draft process as she offered corrections, asked clarifying questions, and provided me with editorial feedback. Finally, I would like to thank Kelley Sirko and Ken Feith at the Metropolitan Archives as well as Beth Odle in the Nashville Room at the Nashville Public Library for their help with images and scanning. Despite my best efforts, there are surely errors and omissions in the pages that follow. I have taken great care to be consistent in regard to written style and formatting as I navigated many iterations of words and phrases throughout the WEHF's history. Any mistakes are unintentionally mine.

Back in May 2013, as I ended my speech, I said, "These memories, this document of life and its history would be lost without words on paper. In a text and Twitter world, it is important to leave behind something tangible, something you can hold in your hand as well as your heart. In short, write it down." With this book the West End Home Foundation has documented the life and legacy of its work—the unsung heroes who helped it succeed and those who benefitted from the organization's commitment to and care for seniors. It is indeed a story worth telling and sharing.

—*Mary Ellen Pethel*

Contents

Foreword

Over 120 years ago, Nashvillians with a passion for caring for our senior population were inspired to create the Old Woman's Home, the forerunner of the West End Home Foundation. That generosity and insight set a standard by which we strive to continue to operate. The original mission of providing direct care for senior women lasted for over one hundred years. Over those many decades, hundreds of women participated on the Board and Auxiliary providing management and financial expertise to the home enabling an even larger group of women to enjoy their final years as residents.

As times changed the Board members were faced with tough decisions regarding the future of the home, but always in the forefront was the loving care of the remaining residents. There is not enough that can be said about those women who saw changes on the horizon and redirected their efforts to enhance the home's original mission. These decisions enabled the organization to serve a much broader senior population through the West End Home Foundation. As President of the current Board of Directors, I am honored to follow in the footsteps of these women that with dedication brought their unique expertise to lovingly serve seniors over the 125-year history. The history of the foundation is dedicated to their perseverance, hard work, and ability to adapt to best meet the needs of Middle Tennessee seniors.

As well as being a source of funding for senior service providers, today we have new opportunities. With a broader perspective, we are in a position to serve as advocates for the frequently silent and underserved senior population and as conveners for the many agencies that support them. We look back at our history and remain grateful for those that had the foresight and commitment to service that led us to where we are today. Thank you to all our past Board and Auxiliary members and staff.

—Kim Sumner Hardin
President, Board of Directors

A Heartfelt
Mission

A Noble Purpose
Origins and Early Years

> " The Nashville Relief Society, one of the most praiseworthy charitable associations of the city, has decided to create a new department giving indigent women a chance to live with dignity.
> —*Nashville Daily American, 1887*

> " To-day we build it for others. In the distant to-morrow this home may very well shelter many of us.
> —*Percy D. Maddin, 1908*

Nashville hosted the National Conference of Charities and Corrections in 1894, the first upper South city to do so since the organization's founding twenty years earlier. It was a major event that signaled Nashville's role as a leading New South city—one that also valued the health and welfare of *all* of its citizens. A key player and reformer who helped to bring the conference to Nashville was Eliza Crosthwaite. As an important member of the local committee, Crosthwaite's credentials included a new Nashville charitable corporation, identified simply as "Old Woman's Home."

Crosthwaite had long served as a leading voice for urban welfare in Nashville. As the city recovered, grew, and industrialized after the Civil War, she emerged as an advocate and social activist for a variety of local causes.[1] In the 1880s, she joined the ranks of the Nashville Relief Society, and it was Crosthwaite who first proposed a residential program to provide room and board for "cultured" elderly women in 1886. With no publicly funded programs at the federal or state levels to help those considered among society's most defenseless citizens, Crosthwaite and other concerned community members began discussing their desire for a private, not-for-profit home. The number of Civil War widows nearing old age exacerbated the need. The following year, Crosthwaite and the Nashville Relief Society published the following in the *Nashville Daily American*:

> It is the province of the Nashville Relief Society to take general cognizance of the distresses of the poor…But it is our duty to listen to calls from people of every condition—the orphan, the widow, the abused and neglected wife, and the stranger who has not a shelter for the night…Therefore, the securing of a large house was decided upon…to more effectively take care of the aged women now under our charge.[2]

The notion that a community or state should bear a responsibility for the care of its aging population gained traction throughout the 1800s, first in the North in cities such as Boston, New York, and Philadelphia. The organizers of Philadelphia's Indigent Widows' and Single Women's Society wrote in 1823: "We were grateful that through the indulgences of Divine Providence, our efforts have, in some degree, been successful, and have preserved many who once lived respectfully from becoming residents of the Alms House."[3] Although such institutions were "designed for those without substantial familial support, these early homes still generally required substantial entrance fees and certificates of good character," according to historian Carole Haber.[4] In other words, private institutional charities established in the nineteenth century were designed to accommodate and provide for a group often identified as the "worthy poor."

As Jeanette Sloan Warner recalled, "As we all know, the Civil War wiped out many family fortunes in the South and took the lives of the heads of the families…Some families were more fortunate and recouped their fortunes in a short time and then there were those who felt the need of a home for widows and orphans."[5] This growing concern for Nashville's elderly women (both widowed and unmarried) with limited assets and options for their twilight years would translate into action starting in 1887. Within two years Crosthwaite was joined by Fannie Battle, Rebecca Porter Howard, Sarah Childress Polk (the widow of President James K. Polk), Samuel and Elizabeth Keith, James and Martha Whitworth, Mr. and Mrs. L.H. Lanier, Judge John Lea, J. S. and Cynthia Reeves, William and Elizabeth Morrow, O. F. Noel, F. W. Waller, Arthur and Agnes Estill Colyar, and other prominent Nashvillians.

The result was the establishment in 1889 of residential space in the Nashville Relief Society headquarters for elderly women of "gentle birth" and "sewing girls" according to early documents. "Sewing girls" were child laborers, typically orphaned or with little family support. For two years, the old and the young lived together in a shelter-like setting. Prior to the passage of the National Housing Act (1934) and Social Security Act (1935), privately operated organizations such as the Old Woman's Home (OWH) offered the best hope for female senior citizens who lacked familial or financial security but who were well-respected citizens with a history of work, church, and/or community service.

A Vision for the Aged

M. H. Howard (Memucan Hunt Howard) was the man whose legacy made the plan for a permanent home a reality. Howard was called a "Nashville capitalist whose name and deeds are an essential part of the history of Nashville's charities."[6] In reality, Howard was responsible for much of the land surveying associated with Tennessee while it was still part of the state of North Carolina. Even after Tennessee achieved statehood in 1796, Howard continued to build his for-

Memucan Hunt Howard. *Image courtesy of Tennessee State Museum, Antebellum Portrait Gallery.*

tune as part of a real estate and land firm known as Hunt and Dickins—securing land warrants, mapping the region, and acquiring tracts (primarily from Choctaw and Chickasaw tribes) that spanned from Memphis to Johnson City. His thirty-year career on the Tennessee frontier ended in the 1820s after his marriage to Rebecca Porter. The couple settled in Nashville where Howard developed and managed several properties in Middle Tennessee.

Historian Pat Wilson summarized that Howard was an astute businessman and humanitarian who made many contributions to Nashville, both in life and death.[7] For more than thirty years, Howard and his wife, Rebecca, were heavily involved in civic issues, education, and philanthropy. Specifically, they were vocal advocates of the temperance movement citing that "drunkenness is… a terrible habit—leading to innumerable crimes and much misery."[8] Howard also served on the Nashville Board of Education from 1856 to 1863, donated land for the building of Howard School, which was named in his honor, and supported other causes that aided women, children, and the working poor. Following the Civil War, he moved to New York and later Philadelphia where he continued to build an impressive real estate portfolio until his death in 1886.[9] M. H. and Rebecca Howard had no surviving children, and based on their philanthropic interests, the couple clearly viewed Nashville as their home.

In his *Recollections of Tennessee*, written three years before his death, Howard stated that for "any poor toiling person, we should benefit them in any way and help a little in encouraging good, and avoiding bad."[10] To this end, Howard bequeathed $15,000 or (2016) $400,000 that led to the establishment of Nashville's first public library, subsequently called the Howard Library. Moreover, his friendship with Samuel Watkins and their combined funds would later establish an independent school, which opened as Watkins Institute in 1885 (today Watkins College of Art, Design, and Film). The Watkins Institute was started for "young men and women who, on account of the necessity of labor during the day, cannot attend public schools."[11]

To address the need for a residential facility for Nashville's elderly females, his Last Will and Testament called for "[t]he establishment of an institution for the care of aged and helpless women who are unable to work and who are without means of support and have no friends upon whom they can call for aid and whose sensibilities would be wounded by the surroundings of an ordinary poorhouse, to which even vice, if attended with poverty, is entitled to admittance, seems to me a much needed charity."[12] He bequeathed approximately $4,000 or (2016) $100,000 to make the idea of such a home financially feasible.

Howard believed a home for older women, who came from respected families and were upstanding citizens, would prevent the indignity of having to live in an institution, called a "poorhouse" or "almshouse." Such institutions emerged during the Industrial Revolution with the purpose of efficiently and cheaply addressing the homeless, orphans, beggars, those unable to work (physical/mental disabled), and other "paupers." To live in a poorhouse was a notoriously cruel and depressing fate—a fate that Howard, and many others, sought to spare for Nashville's elderly women who had no other option if family or friends could not personally care for them.

Howard knew that in order to establish a home for older, otherwise indigent women, additional money would need to be raised. He recognized this explicitly: "More means will be required for such a purpose than I am able to give but I feel it alike duty and pleasure to make a contribution, which the people of Nashville will increase and build such an institution."[13] His actions apparently inspired other leading community members. A small and fragile notebook offers a faded but legible account of gifts:

> It is the intention of the Nashville Relief Society to raise funds for the purchase of a House for the Aged Women and Orphan Waifs now under its care. To this end we the undersigned believing it a noble and worthy object subscribe our names to the following amounts.

Dr. William Morrow	$2500.00
Mrs. Lanier	$1000.00
Judge Whitworth	$600.00
Mr. Robert Warner	$300.00
B.J. Farrar	$250.00
John T. White	$500.00
R.S. Hollins	$100.00
S.J. Slowey	$100.00
Mr. and Mrs. J.S. Reeves	$100.00[14]

So it was that the Nashville Relief Society, one of the city's oldest and largest nonprofit foundations became the parent organization for the "Home for Aged Women and Orphan Waifs," later renamed the Old Woman's Home.

The Nashville Relief Society, established in 1881, was the result of a campaign led by Fannie Battle. Fannie Battle was one Nashville's pioneers in social work who addressed a variety of issues through her activism, passionate service, and lifelong dedication. According to historians Paul H. Bergeron, Stephen V. Ash, and Jeanette Keith she "was brought up to be a genteel southern lady living a quiet life at home. History intervened."[15]

Battle, born in 1842 into a Middle Tennessee middle-class family, lived through harrowing experiences. During the Civil War, she was captured, arrested, and served time in a federal prison for spying after reporting Union positions and activities during the occupation of Nashville after 1862. After the war, engaged to be married, Battle learned of her fiancé's death in a train accident on his way to Nashville for their wedding. Devastated, Battle decided to devote her life to teaching and volunteering with the Methodist church in 1870.

Eleven years later, in 1881, after a flood that left over one thousand people homeless in the downtown area,

Fannie Battle, c. 1900. *Image courtesy of the Nashville Public Library, Special Collections.*

she organized the Nashville Relief Society. Five years later the Board of Directors named her their full-time director, a paid position of power rare for a woman at that time. The Nashville Relief Society would become United Charities after 1901 and eventually was divided into several smaller organizations, one of which

continues to bear her name: Fannie Battle Day Home for Children.

Those involved with urban reform but specifically concerned with the OWH (Old Woman's Home) quickly realized that the city needed a new organization beyond the needs of general relief—an entity independent of the broader Nashville Relief Society. The group, led by Martha Whitworth, Elizabeth Keith, Eliza Crosthwaite, Cynthia Reeves, Fannie Battle, and

Cynthia Reeves.

Elizabeth Morrow, would focus on establishing and maintaining a home dedicated to the security, support, and care of seniors. This accomplished and determined group of women would also form the first Board of Directors and officers.

According to various records, in 1891, the home for "aged women" and the Nashville Relief Society legally parted ways as the "work of each had grown to such proportions as to necessitate their separation."[16] This decision also separated sewing girls and orphans from elderly "gentle women," and made the latter the home's primary focus. Just before the Tennessee State Legislature adjourned for the year (December 17, 1891), lawmakers approved the charter that recognized the Old Woman's Home as a separate nonprofit organization. Martha Whitworth, the wife of Judge Whitworth and a primary backer, explained the organization's leadership structure at a board meeting of the independent Old Woman's Home. The extant minutes report:

Elizabeth Morrow.

> Whitworth explained the 'getting' of the charter, the subsequent appointment of directors, and the raising of the dues to five dollars. She also explained that the ladies who were appointed by the charter members were to become the directors. The charter, having ascertained who the largest contributors were, appointed the directors on that basis...Committees were formed, the new by-laws were adopted. Adjourned.[17]

This event, and the subsequent autonomy it provided, marked the official beginning of the Old Woman's Home—today's West End Home Foundation.

Two Decades in Downtown Nashville

Tasked with the management and operation of the organization, budget, physical plant, and resident application process, the charter members of the Board of Directors immediately set to work. Martha Whitworth was elected the Board's first president, a position she held for eight years. The Board understood the importance of fundraising, and so in 1893 the Young Women's Auxiliary (YWA) was formed to raise money and secure donations for the home and its residents. In addition to funds raised by annual membership dues of $2 for Auxiliary members, the Board of Directors tasked the Auxiliary with sponsoring charitable events to offset the cost of daily expenses related to residents' needs and special occasions. The Board of Directors also procured donations, but did so primarily in the form of large gifts and bequests, which was used to pay salaries, maintain facilities, and purchase property.

In 1892, the ledger proudly reported, "After paying all expenses, there remains 144 dollars in the Treasury." While Whitworth headed the Board of Directors for eight years for the OWH, the financial solvency of the nonprofit was in the very capable hands of Fannie Battle as treasurer and the finance committee. As was usual at that time, men figured predominantly in the structure of the finance committee, but there were at least two women included during these early years.

Martha Whitworth.

Until a permanent home could be found (1889), the top floor of the Nashville Relief Society's office building on Cedar Street served as temporary housing as part of the experiment to expand the relief society's mission to include the care of older women. The first two inmates, as they were called, were Evelyn Cartwright Hall and Nancy E. Lewis. Mrs. Hall died shortly after the move to the new property for the OWH. Mrs. Lewis, the other original inmate, lived only one year after her acceptance in 1889, making her the only resident to pass away before the OWH received its independent charter in 1891.

The purchase of the house at 136 Cherry Street for $12,000 or (2016) $300,000 came about in 1889, from the family of Ben S. Weller, who had owned a tinware business between College and Cherry streets. Frank P. Hume, the secretary of the Nashville YMCA in the 1870s, wrote, "Weller was a strong Union man, and his home was a favorite resort of Union sympathizers."[18] Although Ben Weller died in 1860, his wife, Lucintha, lived in the house until her passing in 1877. Upon her death, the Weller house was sold and rented over the next twelve years prior to its purchase by the Nashville Relief Society (and Old Woman's Home) for the purpose of housing elderly women. Approximately ten women initially moved into the house in 1889.

Old Cherry Street, as this residential downtown district was called, centered on present-day Fourth Avenue North and ran from Broad Street up to Church Street just below the State Capitol. Many of Nashville's most prominent families lived on

Donation from Robertson family to Nashville Relief Society
to purchase Weller House at 136 Cherry Street.

Old Cherry during the mid-1800s. The OWH's Cherry Street neighbors included newspaper man and Unionist, Major E. G. Eastman, the John K. Hume family (Mr. Hume was an auctioneer and businessman), the George Thompson family (operated a dry goods store), the Felix Robertson family (Dr. Felix Robertson was the son of Nashville founder James Robertson), and the Thomas Craighead family.

One notable neighbor was the young William Walker, who had once lived across the street. Walker was a Nashville prodigy who graduated from the University of Nashville at the age of fourteen and later the University of Pennsylvania's Medical College. Walker participated in the Gold Rush of 1848–1849 and in the 1850s attempted to seize territory in Mexico and Central America through a procedure known as a filibuster—a creative legal attempt to claim land by establishing colonies. He was known as "the grey-eyed man of destiny" because of his participation in the Manifest Destiny movement. Walker's ventures were most successful in Nicaragua where his army of mercenaries and local minority tribes seized power in the capital of Granada. President Franklin Pierce recognized the area as a new territory in 1856, but a coalition of Latin American states recaptured it, and Walker returned to Tennessee.[19]

One street west of the Old Woman's Home was Summer Street (present-day Fifth Avenue North). As the OWH women settled into what was called the Weller House, the Union Gospel Tabernacle was under constuction on Summer Street. Funded by Captain Thomas Ryman and later renamed Ryman Auditorium in his memory, the building, completed in 1891, would provide a large venue for religious services and other meetings. The following year the famed preacher Sam Jones brought a revival to Nashville for the building's inauguration. Elizabeth Morrow, Vice-President of the Board of Directors at the time, invited Jones "to hold a meeting at the House," which he did before leaving town.[20] The presence of a one of America's most popular preachers was not only a newsworthy event for the Old Woman's Home but also validated the important work carried out by the newly formed organization.

Residents in front of Cherry Street property, c. 1900. *Image courtesy of the Nashville Public Library, Special Collections.*

Life at the home settled into a comfortable routine after the move to Cherry Street. The Auxiliary and Board of Directors worked together to provide a safe and secure environment for the residents, legally referred to as "inmates." Management accepted ladies over the age of sixty-five based on application and recommendations, a physical examination, and a signed contract agreeing to abide by the home's rules. Women dressed for dinner, received visitors in the formal parlors, played cards, and agreed "not to argue" with other residents. Spinsters and widows, some wealthy and others dispossessed—all shared the common need for assisted living.

In addition to Evelyn C. Hall and Nancy E. Lewis, early residents included Sallie Pike, Judith Percel, Harriet Pickard, Mary A. Bosworth, Annie C. Burney, and Annie E. Frazier. Sallie Pike's birth on June 17, 1809, marks the earliest date of birth found in any of the organizational records. Her life unfolded in the burgeoning days of a newly independent United States. In 1809, Thomas Jefferson had just completed his second term, and James Madison had been inaugurated the fourth president of the United States in March of that same year. The Constitution had been ratified twenty years earlier, and Tennessee was still part of the Western frontier.

Judith Percel was born in 1815, the same year the Treaty of Ghent was signed to end the second war with the British, which began in 1812. Mrs. Percel grew up as Andrew Jackson rose through the ranks of political power, on the state and then federal level, before ultimately ushering in a new Jacksonian Age from 1828 through the 1840s. After the death of her husband with no living family, Mrs. Percel was one of the first women admitted to the "Home for Aged Women and Orphan Waifs," which at that time was still under the jurisdiction of the Nashville Relief Society. She remained in the care of the home for only one year before her death in July 1891 at the age of seventy-six. Another resident with a similar life story was Harriet Pickard. Born on June 21, 1819, she was seventy when accepted as a resident of the newly established home for senior women in 1889. Miss Pickard lived through the move to the Cherry Street location and passed away in 1894.

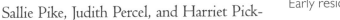

Early resident, Mary A. Bosworth.

Sallie Pike, Judith Percel, and Harriet Pickard serve as prime examples of the limited options for women who could no longer earn a living but had no family with whom to live. The emergence of the Old Woman's Home gave such women the opportunity to live out their remaining years with dignity and love provided by the OWH "extended family." Without such an organization, options were dire: homelessness or an institutional asylum.

Finances and Facilities

Raising funds for the home, and its occupants, was a constant worry for those in charge. In addition to the residents' one-time admission fee of $100 or (2016) $2,600, selling handicrafts and sewing allowed residents an opportunity to give back—with profits divided between the Auxiliary and the inmate. Some knitted or embroidered, while others did heavier sewing such as alterations or dress-making. A Young Women's Auxiliary list of "Cash Received for Inmate's Work" shows one resident, simply referred to as Mrs. Harris, for "sewing fancywork" in 1894. Martha Sloan (born January 12, 1811) was still quilting at age 87, donating her $1 profit to the Auxiliary. An 1897 annual report published just months before her death stated: "Mrs. Sloan, is still living and shedding sun-light in the Home by her sweet Christian spirit. Her work never ceases."[21]

In 1906 a local newspaper reported: "The Home has sheltered seventeen old ladies this year. They have not only been furnished with wholesome food, good clothing and attention, but every effort has been used to give them pleasures also…The past year [the Auxiliary] hosted a linen shower, at which friends of the institution contributed a liberal supply of household and table linen, and $40 in money. The health of the inmates has been good, considering their age."[22] The article concluded that the residents were in capable medical hands with "Dr. Sam S. Bloomstein, who has given free his untiring service, and Dr. Richard W. Dake and other physicians who have responded cheerfully to all calls."[23]

Dr. Matt Buckner was another medical doctor who volunteered as a physician. Even though he was forty-six years old when the United States entered World War I, Dr. Buckner joined the service. Before reporting to Fort McClellan, Alabama, "he went to the home and kissed all the old ladies there."[24] The work of the Auxiliary to raise money and secure donations as well as pro bono services of medical doctors made these women and men unsung heroes in the long-term care and health of the residents.

The first thirty years of the OWH also included a major building campaign. The original property had been purchased for $12,000 with a down payment of $8,000 ($2,500 of which was donated by Dr. William Morrow). By 1895 the remaining loan balance had been paid off, and the home's financial outlook looked secure. The space quickly filled, and the need for senior care continued to grow in the first decade of the twentieth century. As early as 1906, the Board of Directors began discussions to address the need for more room. Local newspaper reports noted, "The directors feel the need of larger quarters to accomplish the work that is possible as many old ladies are waiting to enter the home, and are in need of its comforts, but cramped quarters will not permit it."[25]

The first option for expansion was the construction of a new facility on a lot purchased by the OWH on Church Street. However, after much deliberation the decision was made to move farther west to construct a new residential home. The Church Street lot was sold in 1906, and early the next year the OWH bought a large 800-foot wide lot on West End Avenue near Twenty-Eight Ave-

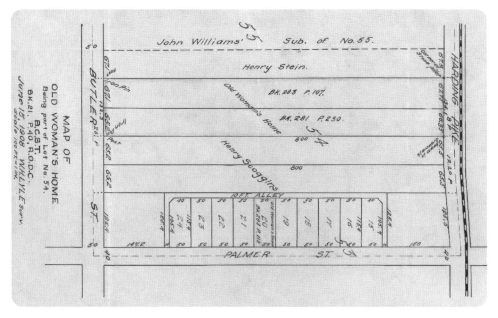

Property record for West End Avenue lot, 1909.

nue for $6,500 or (2016) $175,000. A bequest from Susan McGavock Smith for $16,000 or (2016) $400,000 made the purchase possible, but the OWH first had to survive a legal challenge by Smith's heirs. The court ruled that the "Old Woman's Home is a charitable corporation…and that the property in question for the use and benefit of the Old Woman's Home is valid."[26] Once the case was decided in favor of the OWH, plans for the new buildings moved forward. The main architect was Mr. C.A. Ferguson; however, Mrs. Sara Ward Conley was also a consultant on the project. Conley was a Ward Seminary graduate, designer of the Woman's Building at the Centennial Exposition of 1897, and a supporter of the OWH.[27]

A groundbreaking ceremony on August 12, 1908, marked the new chapter for the OWH. The building committee was composed of prominent local men including John B. Ransom, Walter Keith, Julian Cooley, G.M. Neely, Carter Reeves, and Percy D. Maddin. Maddin, a lawyer, banker, and railroad man (with the Nashville, Chattanooga, and St. Louis Railway) was the husband of Mary Belle Keith Maddin, daughter of President Elizabeth Keith, and Vice-President of the Young Women's Auxiliary (see Chapter 2).

Given his deep ties to the organization, Maddin was chosen as the keynote speaker for the groundbreaking ceremony. After the cornerstone was laid, he walked to the podium and exclaimed: "What a noble institution! What a grand purpose!… When father and husband and children have gone, when their locks are whitened by the snows of many

Cornerstone Box excavated prior to demolition of West End Avenue home.

winters and their faces are furrowed perhaps with sorrow and with years, here they will find a haven of rest." Maddin then pointed to the residents in attendance at the ceremony and said, "It is for these women that this house is being built, for these that this work is being done. To what nobler purpose could the benevolent lend their help…to each of those whom good fortune hath brought beneath its roof."[28]

Following Mr. Maddin's address and the singing of "O God, Our Help in Ages Past," Will Allen Dromgoole, a prolific writer and journalist for the *Nashville American*, read a poem commissioned by the Old Woman's Home for the event. Dromgoole was quite famous and well known throughout the United States—author of over eight thousand poems, over five thousand essays, and thirteen books (including *The Island of the Beautiful* in 1911).[29] Her poem, entitled *House of Love*, began, "We build today this House of Love, For those whose tottering years, Have faced the angry tides of fate, In helplessness and tears," (full poem Appendix A). At the close of the ceremony, Elizabeth Morrow placed within the cornerstone a copper memory box that contained the following items:

- photographs of Board of Directors Presidents Martha Whitworth and Elizabeth Keith
- photograph of Board of Directors Vice-President Elizabeth Morrow
- photograph of the then-current "inmates" living in the home
- copies of the address presented by Mr. Maddin and poem *House of Love*
- names of the lady managers of the home
- brief resume of the notable events in the history of the home
- coins, religious literature, and "souvenirs from the old ladies"
- map of the West End Avenue site

• small loaf of bread "hermetically enclosed in a sealed tin receptacle" in honor of Charles Mitchell whose bakery sent a loaf of fresh bread to the home each day[30]

Approximately eighteen months later, in 1909, builders completed the West End Avenue home near Vanderbilt University at a cost of $23,000 or (2016) $585,000. On the cold and windy afternoon of February 17, 1909, the "old ladies bid farewell to their first home and through the kindness of Mr. Finley Dorris they were taken in horse-drawn carriages to the new building on West End Avenue."[31] What a sight it must have been—ladies waving from the carriages of the Finley Dorris Funeral Home as they proceeded up Broadway Avenue to the West End address.

The new home with its magnificent Ionic white columns and three large porches featured on its first-floor formal parlors, nine bedrooms, a hospital room, medical reception office, director's office, dining room, large reception hall, kitchen, pantry, and china closet. There was only one full bathroom on the first floor. The second floor had twenty-two residential rooms, two full bathrooms, and three porches. The third floor was used for storage. The building featured modern conveniences of the day including "illumination by electricity," a state-of-the-art steam boiler for heating, stationary washstands in each

Nashville Daily American, 1909.

bedroom, and ceiling fans.[32] Modern conveniences would not include private toilets, showers, or air conditioning for another fifty years. The dining room could seat up to one hundred people, and the high ceilings in the hall and parlor were beamed with oak. News reports added, "Beautiful new rugs and old mahogany and rosewood sofas were moved from the old home on Cherry Street."[33] There was not an elevator so residents climbed and descended (with assistance as needed) from a large graceful stairway, which branched at the landing and featured an artistic stained-glass window. This window and the ornate

Foyer and front room of West End Avenue home, c. 1915.

torch represented at its center would become the trademark symbol for the organization and still serves as the present-day WEHF logo.

In order to raise additional funds for furniture and maintenance, the Auxiliary Committee and Board of Directors pursued a strategy that allowed individual rooms to be endowed for $2,500 to $3,000. The endowment of rooms or physical facilities was an increasingly common and creative way to raise funds during a time when marketing and development departments did not yet exist. This began with the Rachel Stockell Fund established with $10,000 or (2016) $250,000. The Stockell Fund helped to endow four rooms. Subsequently, as the campaign continued, friends of the home furnished and maintained many of the rooms as memorials to loved ones.

The admission fee for residents was also raised from $100 to $200 sometime between 1898 and 1906. Despite raising the rate, the one-time fee paid by incoming residents fell far short of covering all living and medical costs for life, as well as final expenses. Thus, the OWH needed substantial fundraising and pro bono services in order to maintain the viability of the organizational model. To meet such financial demands, the institution invested any stocks, bonds, and other assets bequeathed by the residents. The Board of Directors also pooled monetary resources to establish an endowment with approximately $675 in 1914. The endowment was key for the sustainability of the OWH, and indeed continues to sustain the important work of the West End Home Foundation.

Life on West End Avenue

From the 1910s to the 1930s, residents enjoyed a new favorite pastime as they sat in the main parlor and listened to music played on a Victrola, a record player produced by the Victor Talking Machine Company. Based in New Jersey, Eldridge Johnson had worked to enhance the technology and audio quality of Thomas Edison's earlier phonographs. Johnson's new record player was released at the end of World War I (1914–1918). The Young Women's Auxiliary raised funds in 1918 to purchase the new Victrola, and one of the first records given to and played at the home was an Edison Diamond Disc Record. The *Nashville Banner* published an account of the YWA event: "With pronounced success the benefit tea met on Tuesday afternoon…The proceeds derived from the entertainment will be used in purchasing a Victrola for the home, and each guest present donated a record for the new player. Residents from the home, also in attendance, were the honored guests of the afternoon."[34] The feature of the afternoon was a theatrical performance given by a number of the students of Ward-Belmont. Ward-Belmont was an all-girls school that maintained three divisions: college preparatory, music conservatory, and junior college.

Victrola purchased in 1918 by the Young Women's Auxiliary for the residents.

The Victrola was an instant hit with the residents. They listened to

music during tea time and at
night as they read, played cards,
or occasionally danced with one
another—recalling stories from
their glory days. The home certainly maintained a culture of
refinement for these ladies beyond what they could have experienced or afforded on their
own at that point in their lives.

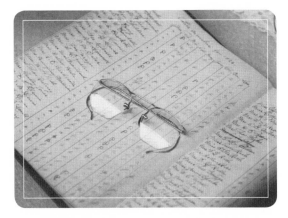

Meeting minutes and roll of Young
Women's Auxiliary, 1918.

The OWH explicitly noted from its beginning that it was "strictly non-sec-
tarian." In fact, in 1908, a printed announcement read that the organization "ap-
peals alike to the Presbyterian, the Baptist, the Episcopalian, the Methodist, to the
Jew and to the Gentile, to Greek and to barbarian."[35] However, religious worship
was encouraged for all residents, most of whom participated. Church services
and Bible studies were held every Tuesday led by a local minister from various de-
nominational churches downtown. There was a religious services committee that
scheduled the services and preachers. A woman listed as Mrs. Richardson came
every Tuesday between 1910 and 1918 to "play the piano accompaniment to the
singing of hymns."[36] This weekly service was a highlight as stated in the *Nashville
Banner*: "This is the only religious service that some of the inmates ever have the
privilege of attending, as they are physically unable to attend church service Sunday morning, and while it is the desire of the management that every woman who
can do so attend these services, it is by no means compulsory."[37]

Within ten years of moving to its West End location, the demand and
need for senior care in Nashville had already surpassed the new building's
capacity. A local newspaper reported in 1918, "At present time every room
in the home is occupied with a single resident and one room with two occupants, and two other rooms for the director and reception room on the

second floor used as bedrooms…There are at present beside the matron, Mrs. Elizabeth Hinton, thirty-four inmates in the home. During the entire time of its twenty-seven years the home has cared for 82 ladies, 48 of whom have gone to their eternal home."[38]

"So smoothly and quietly have the affairs of the Old Woman's Home moved on that it is impossible to realize another year has passed," wrote Mrs. J.L. Watkins in 1918. However, the number of applicants increased significantly in the 1920s. Over the next two years the Young Women's Auxiliary and the Board of Directors would raise and direct funds to build an annex on the home. The lead gift was $10,000 or (2016) $160,000, a bequest by longtime supporter Julian Cooley, and named in his mother's memory.[39] The remaining funds came through additional donations. The 1920 dedication of the Mary Lanier Cooley Memorial Annex marked the home's first expansion after the move in 1920.

The annex was actually an existing structure—the two-story brick home next door. The Cooley Memorial Annex opened after renovations that included the installation of a furnace and electricity, as well as new paint, plumbing, and flooring. The "new" building accommodated fourteen additional persons with single rooms and four rooms large enough for double occupancy. The twenty-ninth annual report captures a picture of the home in 1920: "The two buildings have been connected by a covered passage way, which we have converted into a sun parlor, the side walls being entirely made up of a glass window. When the sun is shining this is an ideal room for the comfort of the inmates, with the furnace heat, easy chairs, and large rug."[40] The sun porch doubled as a long hallway, which also functioned to connect the approximately sixty-feet between the main home and the annex.

Long-term care for seniors in Nashville was not limited to white women, although the OWH's organizational structure made it the most successful. An Old Soldier's Home provided care and shelter for Civil War veterans, and there

Charter Members of the Old Woman's Home, 1891.

was also an Old Colored Women's Home (OCWH). No black women were officially admitted to the Old Woman's Home, though likely none applied given the era of segregation and Jim Crow. The OWH did maintain a charitable and cooperative relationship with the OCWH through donations of medical equipment, clothing, food, and furniture.

While there were no African-American residents at the Old Woman's Home, there were many black women (and men) who worked at the home during its early years as caretakers, cooks, and housekeepers. Notably, many early photographs include black caretakers alongside the white inmates in group photographs, which validated their role as an essential part of the day-to-day life at the OWH. Among them were Mr. and Mrs. Willy (1887–1890), listed as the home's caretakers, and one of the first matrons, Fannie Johnson (1889–1906).[41] They lived on the property in separate quarters during and after their employment. The three were cared for by the home until their deaths.

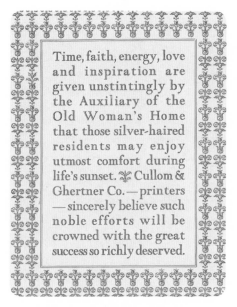

Time, faith, energy, love and inspiration are given unstintingly by the Auxiliary of the Old Woman's Home that those silver-haired residents may enjoy utmost comfort during life's sunset. ❧ Cullom & Ghertner Co. — printers — sincerely believe such noble efforts will be crowned with the great success so richly deserved.

Local support in the form of advertisement, c. 1920.

In just thirty years, the Old Woman's Home evolved from an idea to save elderly women from almshouses into a thriving charitable nonprofit that provided dignity and comfort to the "worthy old."[42] The OWH accepted its first pair of inmates in 1889; by 1920 there were fifty residents and a long waiting list. Impressively, during this period over one hundred women had lived under the care and charge of the Old Woman's Home. The earliest residents shared space with young, single sewing girls and lived in makeshift bedrooms on the top floor of the Nashville Relief Society's office. By 1920, some women enjoyed a private room, entertained guests in the grand parlor, rocked in chairs on the front veranda, and chatted with passers-by on West End Avenue. In November 1893, Fannie Battle had written to Elizabeth Keith to inform her that the treasury had collected $116.07, expended $104.80, and maintained a balance of $11.27. By 1920, the annual budget exceeded $20,000 or (2016) $244,000 with a carried balance of more than $700 and a healthy endowment managed by the Board of Directors and Men's Advisory Board.

From humble beginnings and a noble purpose, the Old Woman's Home rose to meet the need. As Nashville roared into the 1920s, the OWH set goals for growth and a secure future—for organizational finances, as well as the residents. These goals would be tested by changes in leadership, a decade-long economic depression, and a Second World War. 🌿

"Carry on the Work"
Good Times, Hard Times, and Life at the Home

> " The home's future is certain and secure. None need fear that it will fail to carry on the work.
> —*Elizabeth Keith before her retirement in 1924*

> " Their eyes filled with thankful tears, many older than three score and ten, as the overjoyed women accepted gifts with the coyness of teenagers.
> —*Nashville Banner, December 17, 1954*

It truly was a family affair. From 1900 to 1946 two women provided constant and steady leadership for the Old Woman's Home, making it one of Nashville's most successful charitable societies. At the helm from 1900 to 1924 was the formidable and fearless Elizabeth Evert Bellsynder Keith—Lizzie to all who knew her. Her daughter-in-law, Emmy Keith, would lead the OWH from 1924 to 1946.

Before her selection as Board president, Elizabeth Keith served as a Vice-President under Martha Whitworth from 1892 to 1900. Originally moving to Nashville from New Orleans in the early 1880s with her husband, Samuel, her interests included charitable work and urban reform. There she was active in a benevolent society that aided vulnerable and exploited women (of all ages) living in areas such as the French Quarter and Canal Street.

Her grandson Walter Keith Jr. recalled, "The Old Woman's Home was my grandmother's life work and with great respect she called it *The Home*. She visited

Early photographs of Elizabeth (Lizzie) Bellsnyder Keith and Samuel J. Keith, c. 1880. *Images courtesy of Chandler Williams Cartozzo.*

the home at least two times a week. Her carriage man, Hardy, drove her in the mornings and returned to pick her up in the afternoons. I would ride with them and Hardy sometimes let me sit in the box with him. Her existence was her family, her church, and the Old Woman's Home."[1] Lizzie retired from her post on the Board of Directors of the Old Woman's Home in 1924, at the age of 87, in part because of personal health but also to take care of her daughter, Mary Belle Keith Maddin, who was severely ill. Sadly, Mary Belle passed away later that year at the age of fifty-five.

The OWH was not just an organization for Mary Belle, it was an extended family she had known since childhood. As a young woman, she remained active in the OWH organization as did her husband, Percy D. Maddin; the couple led the planning and move to the West End Avenue facility in 1908–1909.[2] For over a decade she was the Vice-President of the Young Women's Auxiliary. Following her death in 1924, the home released a statement: "She has been

Emmie Ewing Keith and Walter Keith, c. 1930.

identified with the home since her childhood, first as a member of the Auxiliary and then later as one of the Board of Directors. Her sweet presence and helpful advice will be missed and her death is a calamity."[3] From the inmates and staff to the Auxiliary and Board of Directors, the retirement of Lizzie and death of Mary Belle was devastating to the entire OWH organization. The sadness continued the following year when Lizzie died on November 14, 1925.

One bright spot remained: Emmy Ewing Keith would pick up the torch of leadership and carry it for the next twenty-two years. Emmy was the wife of Walter Keith, son of Samuel and Lizzie. Walter Keith Jr., her son, remembered his early involvement at the home on West End Avenue: "When Mother became President I became a handyman. Seldom a month passed that I was not called to fix a leaky faucet, unclog a drain, or put a bulb in a ceiling light fixture. My main task, however, was to clean out the flues to the heating boiler. My mother would call 'Son, that old boiler is smoking. Go to the home and try to do a better job this time.' 'Yes mother,' I always replied."[4]

Emmy Ewing Keith would serve just as admirably as her mother-in-law as the President of the Board of Directors from 1924 to 1946. In addition to serving as a general handyman, Walter Keith Jr. also remained involved as an active member of the Advisory Board. The Keith family and others on the Board and Auxiliary would guide the Old Woman's Home through uncertain times. Despite economic depression and World War II, the OWH managed to expand financial investments, purchase additional property, add residents, and increase community involvement.

The Keith women led the organization with vision and purpose for more than fifty years and never lost sight of the OWH's mission of providing basic comfort and care for seniors. As noted in meeting minutes, they exhibited "zealous" and "untiring" efforts to the institution's great benefit. The equally dedicated members of the Board of Directors and Young Women's Auxiliary made such efforts possible.

Men at the Old Woman's Home

In 1922, two years prior to stepping down from the OWH Board of Directors, Lizzie Keith set in motion a plan to create an annex that would serve as a home for elderly men. Admitting men or couples had been a longtime goal of Lizzie Keith, and many on the Board and on the Auxiliary during the home's first forty years agreed with her. The original decision was based on the following proposal, recorded in a 1922 letter from Percy D. Maddin (her son-in-law) to the Board of Directors and Young Women's Auxiliary:

> Amendment One proposes to accept the gift of Mrs. Samuel
> J. Keith of the property recently acquired by her from Miss
> Sarah Scoggins lying next east of the Old Woman's Home

on West End and going back toward Highlands Avenue. Amendment Two thereupon moves that we enlarge and extend our work so as to care for old couples and old men and that we gratefully accept the offer made by Mrs. Keith."[5]

Lizzie Keith, c. 1922.

The motion was seconded and unanimously passed by members of the Advisory Board and the Board of Directors Building and Grounds Committee. Percy D. Maddin filed papers with the county clerk and State of Tennessee to amend the institution's charter of incorporation in order to provide "the necessary power to carry on this additional work."[6] However, the reality of introducing significant numbers of men or couples was never seriously considered. Rather the Board's push to allow couples originated with Keith's recognition that deserving elderly women, and would-be model residents in need of assisted living, should not be denied simply because they were not widowed.

The Keith Memorial Building opened in 1923, and the first couple was admitted in 1931. Orville and Ida Stief Stockell lived together in the home until her passing in 1938. Orville remained in the home until his death three years later. Ida Gower Stief Stockell was the adopted daughter of Mr. and Mrs. Bruno H. Stief, owners of a local jewelry store; her biological parents were Felix Robertson Gower and Mary Fields Gower. Her application was given preference because her family's connections to Nashville—the roots of the Robertson, Gower, and Stief families—ran deep in Middle Tennessee. Ida's biological father was the great-grandson of Nashville founder James Robertson.

Room endowed by Lillie R. Shipp in memory of her husband, Albert W. Shipp, one of two men who lived at the Old Woman's Home.

Her adopted father, Bruno, established the B. H. Stief Jewelry Company in 1858, which served as the city's most prominent shop for watches, jewelry, gold, and silver. Members of these families had also made many donations and bequests to the OWH over the years.[7]

The second couple was admitted in 1934 (Mr. and Mrs. Alfred Shipp). Mr. and Mrs. Shipp were friends of United States Supreme Court Justice James Clark McReynolds, who made a bequest to the Old Woman's Home in their honor. Prior to McReynolds' appointment to the Supreme Court, he had served as the attorney general for President Woodrow Wilson, and his ties to Nashville dated back to 1882 as valedictorian at Vanderbilt University.[8] Alfred Shipp passed away in 1938, survived by his wife, Lily Rountree Shipp, who lived in the home twenty-five more years (d. 1963).

After the death of Orville Stockell in 1941, the Board of Directors determined that the home was not adequately set up to care for aged men or couples. Men as "inmates" changed the home's atmosphere and complicated medical and healthcare needs. After the death of Mr. Stockell, the Board of Directors did not accept any additional men or couples. In the end, while well intentioned, expanding the mission of the organization to include the care of men proved too ambitious. The Old Woman's Home would remain true to its name after 1941.

Surviving and Thriving during the Great Depression

Years earlier, in 1908, President Elizabeth Keith underscored the success of the OWH as a business enterprise:

> "With the passing of years one donation has been followed by another, and these by others, until to-day it stands upon a secure and safe financial basis…[It] can be said that [our finances] are safe beyond the reach of poverty or the possibility of failure. The entire property, including the home, is worth about $60,000, and its annual income from all sources, including donations, is over $3,600."[9]

Fifteen years later, the organization's budget was tight but secure, all debts were met, and the OWH received several bequests. Mrs. Walter Stokes, the

Old Woman's Home prior to opening of Cooley Annex, 1919.

Board of Directors' Treasurer during the 1920s and 1930s stated, "The problem of raising sufficient funds to meet the current expenses from year to year is one that has given us great anxiety, and it seems that the age of miracles is still with us. The faith of our president that somehow the funds to take care of the necessary expenses would be forthcoming, has been more than justified."[10]

The year 1923 provides a glimpse into the OWH's operating budget and expenses prior to the Great Depression. Major expenses included:

Meats, groceries, milk, butter, and eggs	$3,614.20
Ice cream (birthdays are always observed)	$48.60
Coal	$1,029.00
Insurance	$587.00
Servants	$2,092.30
Laundry	$910.00
Drugs	$273.00
Paving	$310.00
Plumbing	$687.00
Repairs	$993.38
Painting	$1,488.00[11]

In addition to detailed expenditures, there were several sources of new funding in 1923 beyond Auxiliary dues, annual donations, and fundraising events. The County Court of Davidson County provided $1,620 in funding, and one of the residents who had received money from a family member, gave $250 to the OWH because "she could finally afford to give back to the place that had given her so much."[12] The final gift to the home that year was the most financially significant in the organization's history since its founding. The death of Jane Eliza Plunket in 1919, and the settlement of her estate over a four-year period, resulted in the fulfillment of her bequest to the OWH in the amount of $52,365 or (2016) $740,000. Plunket was the widow of Nashville's most prominent surgeon turned City Council President, Dr. James D. Plunket. No one would disagree with the conclusion of Mrs. Walter Stokes: "It seems that the parable of the loaves and the fishes is being repeated in our case."[13] Such careful budgeting, the emphasis on increasing the endowment, and the continued cultivation of donor and community relationships would literally pay dividends during the Great Depression.

Decades prior to the Great Depression, as early as the 1870s, Nashville garnered the nickname *Athens of the South* for its institutions of higher education as well as its venues for the performing arts and cultural offerings. By the 1920s Nashville had added the moniker *Wall Street of the South* as a regional center for banking and business. According to historian Don Doyle, "Annual bank clearing for all Nashville banks rose from $323 million in 1915 to $864 million in 1919, then skyrocketed up to $1.24 billion in 1929, up more than 280 percent since 1915."[14] Unfortunately, banking institutions in Nashville and across the nation were engaging in risky behavior with little government oversight, regulation, or consumer/investor protections.

As a result, the Great Stock Market Crash in late 1929 hit Nashville particularly hard because of the local economy's dependence on banking and investments. On November 14, 1929, James E. Caldwell's Fourth and First Bank, which held over $100 million in assets and headquartered in Nashville, announced its insolvency. Luke Lea's Liberty Bank and Trust closed the same day. Nashville slid into a severe depression after these two banking empires fell. Within three years, bank clearings in Nashville had fallen from $1.24 billion to $460 million, a 63 percent drop.[15] The city's churches and charities opened soup kitchens as unemployment rates rose over 15 percent in Nashville from 1929 to 1933. Some in the state legislature even began a campaign to impeach Governor Henry Horton for his connections to Lea and other bankers.

Tennessee was also hard hit as an agricultural state, already in a three-year drought. After 1930 prices dropped significantly for lumber, flour, cotton, and other textiles. Nashville and Middle Tennessee's working class, whether urban or rural, suffered great economic hardship. However, many in the middle and upper class remained insulated from such dire circumstances as most were college-trained, owned property, and maintained some savings or secure investments. Still, as Robert Margo, economist and professor at Vanderbilt University, stated, "The Great Depression is to economics what the Big Bang is to physics."[16]

The severity of the economic depression that began in 1929 only serves to highlight the resiliency of prudential governance by those involved in and connected to the Old Woman's Home. In fact, the OWH's investment portfolio was a model of money management. Careful budgeting, meticulous bookkeeping, and administrative oversight ensured that the OWH lived within its means. In other words, the organization never spent more than it raised and consistently moved larger sums of money, received through bequests and donations, into longer and less liquid investments such as government and large corporate bonds. The home's philosophy, which combined purposeful service and community spirit, proved valuable as the South struggled through the economic downturn of the 1930s.

From 1917 through 1929, the OWH Board of Directors had wisely invested less in the speculative stock market and more in the more stable bond market. Bonds purchased were tied to public utility companies (Alabama Power and Pacific Telephone and Telegraph) as well as industrial and public bonds (US Savings, General Motors, and Standard Oil). Stocks purchased in the 1930s also fared comparatively well against the financial portfolios of institutions and individuals alike. Based on the recommendations of the Finance Committee and Advisory Board, the Board of Directors chose stocks in large blue-chip companies such as Proctor and Gamble, General Electric, Western Union, American Telephone, and Nashville and Decatur Railroad.

The OWH gained some stocks and bonds through estates willed to the home by both donors and residents. In addition, the OWH continued to re-

SUNDAY, JANUARY 17, 1932

Report of Old Woman's Home Indicates Successful Year

Several bequests, the largest of which was $3,500, making possible repairs and improvements at the Old Woman's Home, where seventy-two women were cared for during the year, are items of interest to be found in the annual report of Mrs. A. B. Benedict, secretary to the board, made public today.

Mrs. Benedict's report follows:

"This report is as brief as possible, because it is our earnest desire to have many readers of THE NASHVILLE BANNER read the whole of it. Every taxpayer in Davidson County has a share in the Old Woman's Home and should know their money is expended. Not that the appropriation from the county maintains the home, but it is of great assistance and the home could not get along without aid from the county. The income from our endowment is small, and were it not for the financial assistance of the auxiliary of the Old Woman's Home and generous gifts received from time to time we could not maintain the home. The most touching and remarkable gift which we have received this year was one of $500 which one of our dear old women had saved during many years from a monthly pension. One source of income is our sustaining membership, which we would be glad to see enlarged. Anyone can become a member by the payment of $5 annually.

"Several bequests which you will note in the treasurer's report made possible some very necessary repairs and improvements, particularly in our kitchen and service departments. Mr. and Mrs. Walter Keith received a rising vote of thanks from the board of directors for their careful and efficient planning and execution of this work.

EIGHT ADMITTED

"In spite of the slight enlargement of the home, we are still full to overflowing and there are many applicants begging to come in. Seventy-two women have been cared for during the year. Eight have been admitted and the following seven have passed away: Mrs. Anna Hawkins Fisher, January 16; Miss Mollie Newby, July 29; Mrs. Letitia Pruett Livingston, August 4; Miss Pauline Tavel, September 22; Miss Mary Jane Carver, October 2; Mrs. Lucy James Childress, December 19; Miss Josie Kelly, December 31.

"Mrs. Walter Keith, president, and the board of directors wish to thank the officers of the board and chairmen of standing committees, the matron, nurses and servants of the home for their faithful and capable service which has rendered this a successful year in the home. We are particularly grateful to our advisory board of men, and to the auxiliary of the Old Woman's Home for their invaluable assistance. Above all, we wish to express our heart felt appreciation of the untiring service of our house physicians, Dr. McPheetersGlasgow, Dr. M. G. Buckner, and Dr. W. C. Bilbro, Jr. They make daily visits to our sick with no reward except what they find from the satisfaction of doing a good deed. Drs.

"Religious services are held at the King and Hamilton, Dr. Hilliard Wood, Dr. Boyd Bogle and Dr. P. A. Williams have been wonderfully kind. home on alternate Tuesday afternoons under the direction of Mrs. D. F. C. Reeves, chairman. Dr. Prentice Pugh administers the communion of our Lord once a month and ministers of other denominations take charge on other Tuesdays. These services are very beautiful and helpful.

"Groups of girls from Ward-Belmont bring gifts to the women and provide entertainment; also young people from different churches in Nashville come to cheer the aged and shut-ins. We are grateful to the Tennessee Electric Power Company which donates street car tickets; to Mitchell's who gives us bread; to Anderson's for oysters; to Betty Lou Bakery for cakes; and all other friends who have been so kind and generous.

"The report of the treasurer follows:

"'I beg to report another successful year for the Old Woman's Home. Three bequests have been made, one from Miss Mary Kate Smith of $3,500, another from Mrs. Leona Horn of $2,300 and a third from Mrs. Anna Gwin of $100. Aside from these bequests there have been gifts large and small amounting to $608. The largest and a much appreciated gift was from one of our dear old women who monthly gets a pension. She saved $500 out of this which she gave to the home in grateful appreciation of her good home and the loving care she receives. These bequests have made it possible to add much needed improvements to the home. Following is a statement of money received and disbursed during the year 1931:

"'Total receipts $25,121.59
"'Total disbursements 25,019.52

"'Balance ....$ 102.07

"'I wish to thank all those who have enabled us to carry on, in however small or large an amount. While we have an income, it is entirely inadequate to our needs and were it not for the help we receive from the County Court and the Auxiliary and all the gifts received throughout the year, we could not maintain this worthy charity.

"'Respectfully submitted,
"'MRS. WALTER STOKES,
"'Treasurer Old Woman's Home.
"'January 1, 1932.'

AUXILIARY'S REPORT

"The secretary of the auxiliary submits the following report:

"'The auxiliary of the Old Woman's Home, under the leadership of Mrs. Henderson Baker, has enjoyed a year of useful service, finding great pleasure in the work, and sincere gratification in the interest and cooperation of the public.

"'Monthly committees have visited at the home and sent delicacies to the sick. Floral designs have been sent to the funerals, and cars have been provided to send the sick to their doctors. The birthday of each resident has been remembered with a gift of money and through the kindness of the managers of the local theaters, tickets have been provided for the moving pictures, which have been greatly enjoyed.

"'At the Easter party a plant was given to each of the women and a delightful program was given by a group of children. In May a luncheon for the women of the home was given at the Belle Meade Country Club under the chairmanship of Miss Effie Morgan.

"'In October the anniversary of the founding of the home was celebrated by the annual pantry shower, with a charming program by prominent local artists. At Thanksgiving, the tables were decorated with fruit and autumn flowers, and at Christmas, Mrs. O. B. Washington and her committee filled baskets with fruit and candy for each resident of the home, with a gift of money from the auxiliary and attractive decorations for the dining room.

"'The Auxiliary made no effort during the year to add to the nurse fund by appeal to the public, but was able from the income of the fund to provide $160 a month for the salary of the nurses at the home.

"'The new officers elected for 1932 are: Mrs. Joseph Thompson, president; Mrs. Henderson Baker and Mrs. Walter Hale, vice-presidents; Mrs. Harry Murrey, secretary, and Mrs. M. A. Montgomery, treasurer.

"'MARY WEBB,
"'Secretary.'

"In conclusion, we submit this report to the public according to our by-laws and ask your continued and increased help in caring for these helpless and otherwise homeless old women.

"MRS. A. B. BENEDICT,
"Secretary."

Annual Report of the Old Woman's Home, *Nashville Tennessean*, 1932.

ceive large gifts through bequests, in part, because the organization was well known and respected throughout Middle Tennessee. These monies were added to the OWH budget and controlled by the Board of Directors, which was guided by the Advisory Board. The Advisory Board primarily comprised of insurance and banking executives, invested the home's money in ways that all but guaranteed significant long-term growth. While many of these men might have suffered personal financial losses during the Great Depression, their expertise in developing a financial strategy and advising the Board of Directors proved invaluable for Nashville's most successful charitable corporation.

As a whole, the OWH not only survived financially, but indeed thrived. Families who were integral to the home's finances included the Clemmons, Cheeks, Keiths, McHenry, Craigs, Maddins, and McDonalds. These families provided primary leadership to the Advisory Board, Board of Directors, and Young Women's Auxiliary. While the three groups operated separately, each group was dependent on the other. The Board of Directors and Advisory Board worked together on major (macro) decisions regarding finances, investments, personnel, applicants, and the home itself. The YWA and the Board of Directors worked together to coordinate and provide maximum comfort and joy for the ladies on a daily basis (micro).

One of the home's major expenses that drew from the YWA's budget was used to pay nursing staff salaries. From the early 1900s until 1941 the funds for nursing were largely managed by the Auxiliary, with stock and bond investments in utility and transportation companies. In the 1920s the Auxiliary operated under a separate budget and began investing funds independent of the larger organizational budget controlled by the Board of Directors. The Auxiliary made its first major investment, $500 in Warioto stock, in 1914. The Warioto Cotton Mills was a major textile company located in Nashville. This initial investment was recommended by Spencer McHenry, who served on the Advisory Board. Meeting minutes in 1918 noted that his wife, Carrie McHenry, was the "able chair of finance" of the Auxiliary's Finance Committee from 1914 to 1928.[17] In sum, the McHenrys initiated and led much of the YWA's investment portfolio for over fifteen years.

In 1928 Mrs. Helen Pickslay Cheek succeeded Carrie McHenry as the finance chairman of the Young Women's Auxiliary. Under the guidance of Mrs. Cheek, who was advised by Robert Cheek, the portfolio contents did suffer some unfortunate losses in the early 1930s, but rebounded within a few years and avoided severe deficits. A historical sketch written in 1952 recalled the risk and shift in investment strategy during the Great Depression: "Within a few years, all of our 'nest egg' had been placed in Massachusetts Institute of Technology [MA Investors Trust], and we are greatly indebted to Mr. Cheek for his careful and successful handling of our funds. He has watched the market and invested at the right time. With all of the stock dividends, Mothers' Day offerings, bequests and gifts, we now have income sufficient to maintain three nurses in the home."[18]

In 1930 a new cadre of officers were named to the Young Women's Auxiliary and Advisory Board who also helped to carry the organization through the economic downturn in Nashville and across the nation. In honor of her service, Mrs. J. S. Reeves was named "honorary Vice-President for life." Lillie Morrow Anderson (wife of Judge John McFerrin Anderson) and Mrs. D. C. Scales were elected new Vice-Presidents, and Mrs. A.B. Benedict was named Secretary. The Advisory Board added Dr. McPheeters

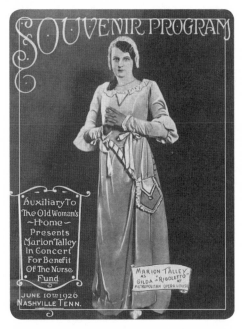

Marion Talley concert fundraiser sponsored by Young Women's Auxiliary, 1926.

Glasgow, Dr. M.G. Buckner, and Dr. W.C. Bilbro. The new Auxiliary officers continued to host specific fundraising events, such as a special three-day benefit at the Parthenon in 1931 and an invitation-only event at Ward-Belmont, in 1932. At Ward-Belmont a comedic routine was followed by a program featuring "dances and musical selections under the direction of Miss Van Houton, who played several piano solos."[19]

The staff budget for the home was one of the top items on the agenda for OWH leaders and committees. The annual salary for nurses paid in 1930 was $2,460 and the salary of the matron, caretakers, and domestic workers totaled over $4,600. The matron of the home, Elizabeth Hinton left in the 1920s and was replaced by Sarah Covington who would supervise and manage the OWH and its residents from the mid-1920s through the early 1940s.

The Young Women's Auxiliary had raised funds to hire and pay for the home's first full-time trained nurse, Julia Bentley in 1918. When Bentley retired in 1930, it became clear that more than one nurse (and nursing shift) was needed to meet the medical needs of the residents. To increase the number of trained nurses and the total nursing fund budget, the Auxiliary purchased bonds in 1930, increased dues to $5, and expanded the number of fundraising events. Because of their efforts, an additional full-time nurse was hired in the mid-1930s.[20]

New Government Program

Another source of income emerged during this period that would help to offset medical and housing costs and provide the home with a regular cash flow. This income came in the form of a new government program authorized by the Social Security Act of 1935, which began payment in 1940. This legislation was intended to provide a safety net for society's most vulnerable citizens, especially those affected by the Great Depression and left behind by an increasingly industrial economy. The purpose of Social Security, also known as Title VII, was as follows:

> An act to provide for the general welfare by establishing a system of Federal old-age benefits, and by enabling the several States to make more adequate provision for aged persons, blind persons, dependent and crippled children, maternal and child welfare, public health, and the administration of their unemployment compensation laws; to establish a Social Security Board; to raise revenue; and for other purposes.[21]

In the 1930s, most state governments and the federal government agreed that the "rising proportion of elderly persons in almshouses was a sign that older people could no longer compete in the modern world," according to Carol Haber in *Old Age and the Search for Security*.[22] Moreover, those with pensions were denied admittance to almshouses or public infirmaries based on the idea that an earned pension provided the financial means to support a person in old age. Therefore, prior to 1935, any person who received a pension was ineligible for care in a public infirmary or almshouse. Reformers such as Homer Folks, a well-known sociologist, welfare advocate, and New York City Commissioner of Public Charities, argued in the early 1900s, "Only about 15 percent of the almshouse population are there because of strict financial need. The others are physically infirm and sick, and have various kinds of ailments that require personal attention of the kind that you could not get in an individual home."[23] Writing in 1936, following the passage of the bill, economist and later Georgia Senator (1949–1967), Paul H. Douglas stated:

> The dislike for institutional care, has commonly been carried too far, so that there is movement to prevent the pensions from

being paid to those who are in any private institution for the aged…The truth of the matter is of course there is a large group who need the skilled and specialized care which only an institution can present…This can commonly be furnished more effectively in a home for the aged or an infirmary than in the private home or lodgings of the aged person.[24]

Private but nonprofit institutions like the Old Woman's Home in Nashville had long recognized the need for long-term care for women who were not eligible for a public care facility because of monetary assets or pensions. This was part of the brilliance of the founders' vision—to establish a home that cared for elderly women in need, whether they had money or not. It should be noted that the OWH did receive approximately 3 percent of its funding from local taxpayers through Davidson County, but there were no state or federal subsidies until the implementation of the Social Security Act.

Mary Anne Davis, one of the first residents to receive Social Security. Davis passed away in 1943.

Because most families were dependent on male wage earners at that time, Congress enacted legislation in 1939 that "provided benefits for aged wives and widows, young children of retired and deceased workers, young widows caring for a child beneficiary, and dependent parents of retired and deceased workers," according to former Social Security Commissioner Martha McSteen.[25] Following passage of these legislative amendments, monthly payments commenced in January 1940. The first Social Security recipient was a woman much like those in the care of the OWH in Nashville. Ida

May Fuller, born in 1874, had been a teacher and legal secretary in Vermont, working for sixty-five years. Unmarried with no children, she was dependent on meager savings and the generosity of her niece, with whom she lived in Brattleboro, Vermont. Her first Social Security check was for $22.54, and Miss Fuller's assigned number was 000-00-001.[26]

The residents of the OWH also began receiving payments in 1940. The OWH Board of Directors passed a policy in 1941 that Social Security payments were to be turned over to the home in order to sustain long-term financial stability and success while continuing

Nannie Williams Collins, one of the first residents to receive Social Security. Collins passed away in 1941.

to provide quality care. The inmates (as they were still called through the 1940s) of the Old Woman's Home signed over their Social Security checks and were given, in return, a small allowance based on a percentage. Income from the government represented a sort of rent payment from the resident to the OWH. This new income also helped ease some of the fundraising burden borne by the Board and Auxiliary.

By 1950 nearly all of the residents were Social Security recipients. None of the ladies living in the home during this period had contributed directly to this government savings program as laborers, so Social Security payments were small. Still, Social Security helped with the home's expenses in the short term, and this new program would also mark the beginning of a new national approach to senior care. In the 1940s and 1950s public almshouses and infirmaries declined in number as federal subsidies for public institutions that serviced the needs of the elderly decreased. Social Security also allowed for greater financial stability for those over the age of sixty-five, which decreased the need for institutional care.

Another change occurred in the late 1930s and 1940s that raised receipts for the OWH was the admission fee for residents. Unchanged for decades, the previous $100 flat admission fee shifted to a three-tiered system. In 1939, the entrance fee was raised to $500 for Davidson County residents, $750 for Tennessee residents, and $1,000 for those admitted who lived out of state. In 2016 dollars these amounts, adjusted for inflation, equal $8,681.76; $13,022.64; and $17,363.53 respectively. Admission fees were often paid by local churches or even waived if the applicant did not have the money. In 1947 the fee for admission to the Old Woman's Home was increased again but returned to a $1,500 flat rate for all residents, (2016) $16,234.51. The main reason for this decision was a result of additional changes made to Social Security after World War II.

A new Advisory Council on Social Security, formed by the Senate Committee on Finance reaffirmed in 1947: "Since the interest of the whole nation is involved, the people, using the government as the agency for their cooperation, should make sure that all members of the community have at least a basic measure of protection against the major hazards of old age and death."[27] Reforms included in the council's recommendations expanded coverage, increased benefits, and lifted eligibility restrictions for workers as well as the Old-Age and Survivors Insurance (OASI) program. Thus, amendments were passed by Congress to the original Social Security Act and signed into law by President Dwight Eisenhower. These amendments, which strengthened the program through payroll taxes, made Social Security all the more important to both the elderly and the larger economy. The average monthly beneficiaries' number grew from 222,000 in 1940 to over 3 million in 1949.[28]

Even with rising fees of the OWH and Social Security, the waiting list for admission to the home grew in the 1940s and 1950s, due in large part to the quality of care received, amenities, and sense of community when compared to other options for single or widowed senior women. Even getting on the waiting list was quite a process. A potential resident's application often included a personal recommendation by a Board member or someone connected to the organization. Most often applicant referrals came to the Board via a woman's employer, church, or family.

Life at the home for residents before and after the economic depression and the passage of the Social Security Act remained one of comfort punctuated by special occasions. Birthdays were celebrated monthly from 1920 to 1940, when parties were scaled back to once per quarter. Other festive celebrations included Mother's Day, Easter, Thanksgiving, and the Fourth of July. The annual Christmas party at the Maxwell House remained the biggest event of the year (see page 52).

The 1930s also brought two very special guests to Nashville. President Franklin D. Roosevelt came to Nashville in 1936 for the funeral of Speaker Joseph Byrns of the House of Representatives who represented Tennessee's Sixth District. While in Nashville the President made several stops including

Holiday dinner, 1935.

Franklin D. Roosevelt and Eleanor Roosevelt, 1933.
Image courtesy of the Library of Congress.

Ward-Belmont School just off Twenty-First Avenue and very near the Old Woman's Home. Many Nashvillians lined the streets to get a glimpse of FDR, and it was the talk of the OWH in the days that followed. Two years later, Eleanor Roosevelt came to town, giving the keynote address for the Girl Scout Council of Nashville and to accept their designation "Honorary President of the Girl Scouts."[29] Her speech was entitled "The Relationship of the Individual to the Community," and several of the OWH's Auxiliary and Board of Directors members who were also involved with the Girl Scout organization attended.[30]

The Young Women's Auxiliary scheduled excursions for the residents as well. They attended shows at the Ryman and Vendome Theaters, visited the State Fair, and regularly went to the movies with complimentary tickets from

Tea at Fairview sponsored by Auxiliary to collect donated china, silver, linens, and flatware.

local movie houses. If urgent health, transportation, or miscellaneous needs arose, residents could access funds in the Blessing Box, which was established in 1936. Funds available in the Blessing Box typically ranged from twenty to fifty dollars. There were also many trips to the "new" art deco-styled Post Office (today's Frist Center for the Visual Arts) on Broadway completed in 1934. When the weather permitted, and especially during the hot summer months, they sat and rocked on the sweeping front porch veranda of the West End Avenue residence.

Day-to-day, the women enjoyed a served breakfast, lunch, and supper— wearing dresses, pearls, and white gloves for evening meals until 1940. Donated china and silver service were also used for many meals, giving the home an air of formality for these gentlewomen. In the afternoons, they played bridge and checkers; worked on crosswords and other puzzles; read books, magazines, and newspapers; and entertained guests. While not every resident had regular visitors, every visitor became family to the women in the home.

Residents watching the first television in the Old Woman's Home
(left) and Rosa Dail and the Old Woman's Chorus (right), 1952.

The late 1930s through the 1940s also witnessed a new on-campus group
organized by the residents themselves. The Old Woman's Home Chorus prac-
ticed monthly, though more often during the holiday season and prior to scheduled performances. Choristers included women such as Pearl Nineva Cornwell
Hall, who was admitted in 1936 (six years after her husband's death) and lived
for thirteen years at the OWH. Hall enjoyed signing soprano and attended
the Church of Christ connected to David Lipscomb College. The group was
known for its renditions of "old songs" such as the "Bells of St. Mary's," hymns
such as "Amazing Grace," and folk ballads such as "Swing and Turn Jubilee"
and "Whistle, Daughter, Whistle."

The Old Woman's Home Chorus, directed by Mrs. Lorena Armistead Stebbins, featured more than twenty members in the mid-1940s. Stebbins was born,
married, and raised her children in Nashville. She was employed for more than
thirty years as a seamstress before her second husband passed away. Mrs. Stebbins, admitted in 1936, was known for her beautiful voice. On at least one occasion, she set down her conducting baton and sang as the featured soloist. Other
dedicated members of the group included Rosa Dail, Mary Shields, Sadie Marlin, Effie Hart, Mary Vollie Warfield, Eva Little, Eva Collier, Rebecca Harper,

Lizzie Reggins, Mary Davis, Lottie Spire, Minnie Weaver, Nelle Robertson Cannon, Lily Shipp, Perry Smiley, Viola Thompson, Emma Skaggs, Emma Cox, Adelia Rigg, Willie Lovell, Mary Scales, Rachel Harris, Nora Cook, Laura Murphey, and Sallie Moody.[31] The group did not officially disband but rather stopped major public performances in the 1950s. That is not to say that there was any less music in the home. Between playing records and piano and the many school and church ensembles that visited the home—there was often a song in the air.

Old Woman's Home on the Homefront

In May of 1941, a Second World War raged in Europe, but the United States had not yet joined the fight. With newspapers and radio as the main forms of information, the ladies at the Old Woman's Home were engaged with world affairs but largely unaffected by the multi-front war overseas as they celebrated Mother's Day that year. The occasion featured a festive lunch, flowers, and prizes for the oldest mother and mother with the most children. Six months later the country's mood drastically changed when the United States declared war after the Japanese attack on Pearl Harbor on December 7, 1941. The events of the next four years would affect the tone and tenor of life at the home as well as the OWH organization as a whole.

One journalist quipped that war swallowed up the 1940s. And indeed it did. World War II and the draft generated a patriotic spirit of service and sacrifice for families on the home front as nearly half a million young women and sixteen million young men served and fought to protect the United States, preserve democracy in Europe, and retaliate against the Japanese. Nashville's women on the home front also did their part. After a call for nurses' aides, five hundred Nashville women signed up. Among the group were some younger members of the Auxiliary and the home's nursing staff.[32] More than two thousand women from Nashville, including some connected to the OWH, formed the Civilian Defense Council (CDC), which served as a citywide operation. The CDC organized the city into sections, assigned block leaders, published newsletters, and alerted the general public when supplies or volunteers were needed.

The Tennessee State Welfare Department distributed free Victory Garden seeds to the state's senior citizens, and out of sixty thousand families in Davidson County, an estimated fifteen thousand households grew Victory Gardens in 1942 and 1943.[33] The ladies at the Old Woman's Home did their part—clearing a section of their flower garden to plant a Victory Garden. The residents, along with the help of the Auxiliary and the home's staff, grew tomatoes, lettuce, carrots, cucumbers, okra, corn, and beans.

There were also numerous salvage drives in Nashville, particularly in 1942 as the U.S. war effort launched full force on multiple fronts. While the Nashville Boy Scouts collected 50 tons of paper, a citywide rubber salvage yielded 680 tons of rubber in a month. In another three-week drive, homemakers and cooks saved 10 tons of grease and cooking fats that contained glycerin, a key ingredient used in explosives. OWH residents contributed to the patriotic effort and rounded up scrap metal and old keys that contributed to the 44 million pounds of salvageable metal from Davidson County residents.[34] The war also brought members of the Auxiliary, Board of Directors, and the OWH residents together as they joined forces to support the soldiers and volunteered in various capacities with the Red Cross—specifically the Knitting Division and First-Aid Kit Division.

Volunteers Fold Christmas Seals

Volunteers from the Old Woman's Home fold Christmas seals and care packages during WWII.

In May of 1942, Francis Muse Izlar, one of the home's nurses, appealed to *Tennessean* readers to contribute to war efforts on the home front, regardless of age:

> To readers who have passed the years of greater usefulness, yet who desire to have a part in our all-out struggle for survival, I would like to tell some of the activities of the members of the Old Woman's Home. A number of the ladies are active in Red Cross work, knitting sweaters, helmets, socks, and wristlets. Two ladies have finished their hundred hours of work and are wearing with pride the pins awards. Others…have worked faithfully on "Bundles for Britain."
>
> There is work for all of us. Material help in no way fills up the measure of our giving. Refraining from unconstructive criticism…made against our leaders is also a priceless contribution. Our leaders are engaged in a prodigious undertaking…and are human even as you and I.

Nurse Francis Izlar ended her letter with one last piece of advice:

> Even if your hands are feeble and your eyes are dim and the tasks of life are too heavy for you, there is never a heart too old and spent to send out wave upon wave of prayers for God's stricken humanity in occupied lands and for the thousands of brave soldiers who are offering their lives that you and I may be privileged to continue our way of living.

One resident who was immediately inspired by the war-related activities of her new "family" was Mollie Shook. Following the death of her husband, Shook was accepted as a resident in 1942, and lived in the home for twenty-two years. Mrs. Shook not only joined the effort during World War II but rose to the rank of Chairman of the Sewing Unit of the Red Cross—a position she held for twenty years. In 1945, Shook wrote to the *Tennessean*, which published her article "Give Three Cheers." An excerpt of her piece reads:

> On West End Avenue is a home for retired and widowed ladies, called the Old Woman's Home, inappropriately named, however, for many of us are not old but quite young in our activities and spirit. Many of the ladies sew, knit, and crochet, while others are in engaged in Red Cross work of various kinds. The "money jar" is placed on a table in the living room and the ladies make their voluntary contributions as they can. There are 61 of us, and we have contributed $61.54 to the war. Don't you call this "sacrificial patriotism?" Jesus said of the woman who gave her "mite" that "She hath done what she could; she has given her all." Let's give these fine, generous ladies three cheers.[35]

Instead of filling spaces and fundraising for new residents, OWH leadership redirected certain fundraising and food/clothing drives to benefit the war effort rather than the OWH. This allowed the Board of Directors and Auxiliary to reduce expenses as well as devote time and energy on volunteer war efforts. As a result, the total number of residents decreased from sixty-four to fifty-two residents from 1941 to 1948. While many of the Auxiliary's war-related efforts focused on raising money to support the Allies in Europe and in the Pacific, they did seek in-kind donations for the home such as a piano, furniture, new mattresses, rugs, blankets, draperies, and electric appliances. The residents of the Old Woman's Home also continued to receive a variety of pro bono and donated services including complimentary rides for errands and outings provided by Carter Dorris, who owned a car and ambulance service, and season tickets to the Nashville Symphony.

Throughout this era, providing a pleasant atmosphere was still important to those directing the Old Woman's Home, as evidenced by the little things. For example, in 1928, pear and apple trees had been planted behind the home, and an "attractive arbor for grapes was built."[36] During the war, in addition to the Victory Garden, the flower garden was expanded with the financial help of the Centennial Club and Big Brothers of Nashville. In the

Residents on Mother's Day, 1941.

spring of 1942, Mrs. J. E. Scales and Maude Payne filled baskets with beautiful flowers from the home's spacious garden and placed flower arrangements in the rooms of residents who were bedridden.[37] The extensive garden featured something nearly all year. In late winter and early spring there were daffodils, crocuses, and tulips. Springtime brought flowering dogwoods, irises, and white and pink peonies. And in summer, the garden burst with "vibrantly colored" crape myrtles, geraniums, daisies, heirloom roses, hydrangea, and other annuals and perennials.[38]

That it was a different time, there is no doubt. From the post-Civil War era to the post-World War II era, families lived quite differently from today's twenty-first century standards. With more children and fewer options for retirement, many families lived in extended arrangements—with multiple generations under the same roof. When holding a job was no longer possible, many older adults simply moved in with family members. Providing for one's family was a point of pride or honor or both, particularly in the South. This contrast was on full display after a 1941 *Tennessean* article that featured a front-page photograph of residents at the Old Woman's Home. The article discussed the comforts of home enjoyed by the ladies and the important work of the organization to provide such facilities and care. Days later, a letter to the editor was published that read, in part: "I would never allow my mother to go to an Old Woman's Home no matter how much 'refinement' was there, as long as I have a roof over my head, and a hoe-cake in the kitchen. And I certainly hope I don't live long enough to see my children treat me in that manner."[39]

Many in the community responded in defense of the OWH and the residents who lived there, chiding the anonymous editorialist who had criticized the organization that had helped so many. However, the best response came from one of the residents who identified herself as "A Proud Mother of the Old Woman's Home." The OWH resident wrote, "When I read the criticism in the letter signed 'Mother and Daughter,' I did not become angry...for I realized that they were ignorant. Many in our home...have means but did not wish to care any longer for their houses, so turned them and other property over to the board." The editorial continued by making clear that residents *chose* to apply and live as part of the OWH organization and also issued a warning: "Unlike 'Mother and Daughter,' none of us care to be in the homes of our children when a place like this opened its doors to refined, cultured ladies. Look out 'Mother and Daughter.' I prophesy that one or both may spend your last days in some home, but it will not be ours, for you would be a misfit among the ladies here."[40]

Christmas at Maxwell House

The weight of the Great Depression and World War II, which spanned a total of fifteen years, finally lifted after 1945, and Emmy Keith retired the following year at the age of 74. She had faithfully guided the organization through tumultuous times, and would enjoy six years of retirement before her death on December 16, 1951. With her passing, the OWH lost another great leader, and, as the *Tennessean* reported, "Nashville ha[d] lost a respected and useful citizen and member of a prominent Southern family." The paper's tribute to her life was fitting: "Although her name is most closely associated with the Old Woman's Home... numerous other church, civic, and social organizations were fortunate enough to number her among their membership. It can be said that all of them profited from her interest and participation. With all others who knew and admired her, we mourn the passing of this noble woman."[41]

The late 1940s and 1950s would bring a sense of renewed joy and hope to the residents, Auxiliary, Board of Directors, and staff. The number of staff members was increased to ten after World War II, including two full-time nurses (paid by the Auxiliary). Mrs. Eugene Haynes replaced Sarah Covington as the home's superintendent (formerly matron), and resident occupancy was increased from fifty-six in 1945 to more than seventy women by 1958.[42] But nothing reflected the victorious mood felt by the OWH organization, and in Nashville more generally, than the "new and improved" Christmas party organized by the YWA and sponsored by the Board of Directors.

The OWH had long held a special dinner at Christmas for the ladies, which in 1924 was clearly a culinary delight. One of the residents described the meal:

> "The tables fairly groaned with the good things of the season—turkey so tender that our appetites clamored for more, fruits with their colors of orange, purple, and crimson; celery crisp and appetizing; potatoes like foam in their whiteness; cake of varied beauty and richness, with all the added luxuries that one's mind could suggest—a dinner fit for a king, and better than all, provided by love."[43]

The resident concluded, "It was a day of cheerfulness of warmer feeling and deeper appreciation and of sincere gratitude, not only for the one day, but for all our days of comfort at the Home."[44]

Merry Christmas . . . and A Happy New Year

from

The Ladies at the Old Woman's Home

Mrs. Mattie Anderson	Mrs. George Farrell	Miss Hattie May	Mrs. Lillie R. Shipp
Mrs. Geo. W. Andrews	Mrs. E. Y. Fitzhugh	Miss Maggie McCormack	Mrs. Mollie Wright Shook
Mrs. Mary R. Armstrong	Mrs. Annie Graham	Mrs. Laura McDaniel	Miss Pennie E. Smiley
Miss Frances Arnold	Mrs. Wilton Haggard	Miss Lura Anne Merrill	Miss Lottie Spire
Mrs. Mollie Averitt	Mrs. Charles Hall	Mrs. Sallie Moody	Mrs. Jennie Stevens
Miss Loula May Bell	Mrs. William Hart	Mrs. W. D. Mooney	Miss Lelah Stewart
Miss Mary Cason	Mrs. J. B. Hays	Mrs. Anne Rankin Murrey	Mrs. Lena W. Trabue
Mrs. Lula Cox Coldron	Mrs. Ruby Y. Herrin	Mrs. Jo Bennett Northern	Mrs. W. W. Tullos
Mrs. Nora Cook	Mrs. Cora Huckaby	Mrs. George Oman	Miss Effie Wadley
Miss Rosa Dail	Miss Annie Hudgins	Miss Laura Brown Robertson	Mrs. Mary A. Warfield
Mrs. Erle Drake	Mrs. C. A. Jones	Mrs. Mary Scales	Mrs. Robert Warfield
Mrs. Hester Duggan	Mrs. Corille M. Jones	Mrs. Mary N. Searle	Miss Eudora J. Williams
Miss Kate Edmunson	Mrs. Cora Payne Kallock	Mrs. Tennie B. Sharpe	Mrs. Alta H. Wood
Mrs. W. P. Emerson	Mrs. Eva Little	Mrs. Susie Gray Shields	Mrs. L. B. Worley
Miss Mary Falconette	Miss Sadie Marlin		

Christmas Party invitation and residents menu, 1951.

The post-Depression, post-war era would add a new flair to this holiday tradition—one that thrilled residents and featured the organization on a more public stage. From 1947 to 1960, what had been a festive Christmas luncheon turned into an all-day affair and entertainment showcase with Nashville society in attendance. The party was held at the famed Maxwell House located downtown and hosted by Bob Condra—local businessman, real estate developer, and then-new owner of the historic hotel and restaurant. The annual event was fun for everyone involved and was heavily covered by local newspapers. The anonymous columnist, "Betty Banner," writing for the *Nashville Banner* reported in 1951: "Bright and early Tuesday morning, dressed in my most gala bib and tucker, [I went] to catch a glimpse of the 'young ladies' of the Old Woman's Home as they were whisked away to the Maxwell House Hotel by the members of the Board of the Home to attend their Christmas luncheon party."[45] Once at the hotel, Bob Condra, also known as Nashville's "host extraordinaire," and an announcer from the radio station WMAK, "combined forces to make the party a memorable occasion."[46]

Each honored guest (resident) was presented with an orchid by Condra and a gift; however, the real treat came when each lady was paired with a blind date. The "dates" were prominent Nashville men—most of whom were connected to the OWH either as spouses of the Board of Directors or YWA or as members of the Advisory Board. In 1952, the front page of the *Nashville Banner* led with the headline, "Ladies of 80 See Santa," providing a full spread of coverage: "Nashville and Davidson County lawyers, bankers, newspapermen, and merchants 'cheated' on their wives today—but with their spouses' permission. The

> ### ROASTS.
> ADAM COE'S XMAS BEEF, WITH POTATO CROQUETTES.
> Suckling Pig, a l'Anglaise.   Loin of Veal, Madeira Sauce.
> HART & HENSLEY'S (New) C. C. C. HAMS, CHAMPAGNE SAUCE.
> Young Capon, Giblet Sauce.   Domestic Ducks, with Jelly.
> Saddle of Kentucky South Down Mutton, with Red Currant Jelly.
> Green Goose.   Stuffed Young Turkeys.
>
> ### GAME.
> Leg of Cumberland Mountain Black Bear, Sauce Poivrade.
> Tennessee Opossum, Baked with Sweet Potatoes, Old Virginia Style.
> Kentucky 'Coon, Devil's Sauce.   Roasted Quail, au Natural.
> Saddle of Minnesota Venison, with Red Currant Jelly.
> Canvas-back and Red-head Ducks.   Blue-wing and Wood Ducks.
> Roasted Wild Turkeys, with Cranberry Sauce.   Wild Goose.
> Young Prairie Chickens, Broiled, Steward's Sauce.
> Broiled Pheasants, a la Maitre d'Hotel.   Roasted Mallard Ducks.
>
> ### Vegetables.
> Baked Sweet Potatoes.   French Green Peas.   Stewed Tomatoes.
> String Beans.   Yarmouth Corn.   Mashed Irish Potatoes.
> French Asparagus, Butter Sauce..   Oyster Plant.   Succotash.
>
> ### Pastry.
> Mince Pie.   New England Pumpkin Pie.   Peach Tartlets.
>
> ### Puddings.
> English Plum Pudding, Sherry Wine Sauce. Indian Pudding, Cold Sauce.
>
> ### Small Pastry.
> Lady Cake.   Wafer Jumbles.   Jelly Drops.   Yellow Cocoanut Drops.
> Rosalind Cakes.   Sliced Fruit Cake.   Pound Cake.
>
> ### Confections.
> Peach Candy. Almond Drops.   Peppermint Drops.   Cream Bonbons.
> English Walnut Bonbons.   Gum Drops.   Chocolate Caramels.
> Rose Cream Almonds.   Candy Mottoes.   French Mixed Candies.
>
> ### Ornamental Pieces.
> Black Cake.   Almond Macaroon Pyramid.   Fruit Cake.
> Lady Cake.   Jelly Cake.   Italian Marble Cake.
>
> ### Jellies and Creams.
> Charlotte Russe.   Russian Jelly.   Maraschino Jelly.
> English Cream.   Apple Brandy Jelly.
>
> ### Fruits and Dessert.
> Malaga Grapes.   Almonds.   Pecans.   English Walnuts.   Apples.
> Figs. London Layer Raisins. Oranges in Sherry Wine.   Green Gages.
> California Apricots.   Pears.   Dates   Pine Apples in Champagne.
> Vanilla Ice Cream.   Frozen Roman Punch.   Bananas.
> ENGLISH BREAKFAST TEA.   FRENCH COFFEE.

Maxwell House Christmas Party menu, 1949.

gala occasion was affable Robert M. Condra's fifth annual Christmas party and the men, numbering more than 50—were the aged women's dates for the afternoon at the Maxwell House shindig."[47]

At the 1952 party, businessman Ray Ligon asked his dinner date, Frances Arnold, "What do you enjoy most about this party?" The eighty-five-year old Frances exclaimed, "The men!" Loula Bell was the "kid of the group at 66-years old," and one partygoer took one look at Miss Bell and her date, F. C. Sowell, and said, "You not only look younger than Sowell, but you have much more hair."[48] Sally Moody, who at ninety-three years of age was the "oldest gal" at the 1952 party, asked her date, Lynn Meek if he was taken. "He says he's a bachelor," said Sally. "I bet he tells every girl that," she added as she turned to Walter Diehl.[49] Other men who served as dates during these years included John

WMAK announcer and Cora Fitzhugh, 1950.

Teas, retail-owner John Sloan, R.J. "Red" Bottom, real-estate executive Glenn Bainbridge, and Milliner George Kittril.[50] Their wives were members of the Auxiliary and the party's organizers.

Described as "one of the most fun parties of the Nashville holiday season," the event served several purposes. The party recognized the ladies of the home, celebrated Christmas, generated publicity for the OWH, and raised money for the home. The Board of Directors' presidents sponsoring the party during these years included: Lale L. Murrey (1946–51), Elizabeth Estes Kirkman (1951–53), Mrs. Lawrence Howard (1953–55), and Sarah Stevenson (1955–57).[51] However, it was a Young Women's Auxiliary committee that worked behind the scenes for months to organize the event, book entertainment, secure donated gifts, and plan the meal and décor. Among the nearly two hundred guests of the extravaganza during these years included approximately forty of the home's residents, their escorts, donors, and members of the Board of Directors and Young Women's Auxiliary.[52]

There were also countless prizes presented: oldest, youngest, most grand-children, oldest unmarried, married the most times. With over eighty years of church membership, Sally Moody received the award for "longest church atten-dance" for five consecutive years. Presenting the award was Dr. Prentice Pugh, Rector of the Episcopal Church of the Advent—located at that time on the corner of Seventeenth and Edgehill avenues. Pugh served as a surrogate pastor for the home for nearly forty years (1916–55).

The prizes and categories grew more creative as the years passed. As reported in 1954: "Age took no back seat to youth when it came to a waist-measuring contest conducted by Cherry near the end of the program. Taking the prize with the smallest waist among the 44 [attendees] was Miss Loula Bell. Her waistline, girls—28 inches." And when it came to the biggest waistline, Miss Lula Coldron stepped up proudly to claim her title. She said she "wasn't afraid to tell that her waistline was 39 inches." "After all," Lula said, "I'm no spring chicken."[53] Finally, an award was given for the person "still having most of her own teeth," and the prize was a chewy candy bar.[54] Regardless of the winners, "every honored guest departed laden with gifts."[55] One of the ladies, "hugging tightly the gaily wrapped presents, said, 'If only every day would be like this for us.'"[56]

The afternoon also featured an appearance by none other than Santa Claus. The bittersweet memories as-sociated with the holiday season were on full display: "Penetrating the hush were tucked white tissues here and there being raised to the eyes to clear

Sallie Moody and Dr. Prentice Pugh, 1951.

away a stray tear brought on by the memories of many other Christmases. But the arrival of Santa, played by Wilbur Sensing, brought them all back to 1954, and the laughs and cheer he had for all."[57] Another account stated:

> "Forty-four ladies were young at heart once more yesterday, mingling with Santa Claus and the effervescent fervor of Christmas and all its goodness. To them, the many years of their individual lives stepped aside for several hours of partying at the Maxwell House to exhibit a youthful spirit that would have stopped anyone in the world from asking, 'Is there a Santa Claus?'"[58]

In 1952, Mrs. George Oman walked into the room, saw the decorations, food, and Wilbur Sensing as Santa Claus and said, "Lands alive! Did you ever see anything as lovely as all this? It makes you feel so young again."[59] Following the presentation of gifts and dinner, those in attendance were treated to a program of music and dancing. In 1952, radio personality Hugh Cherry was the emcee, and guests enjoyed the performances of such local stars as "cutie-pies Anita Kerr and Dottie Dillard, the talented Bob Johnstone, Herschel Martin, and magician Jimmy Sanders." Dean Durham masterminded and transcribed the program for radio, later broadcast on WMAK. Durham stated, "It was sheer pleasure personified."[60]

Lena Trabue and WMAK emcee, dance at the Maxwell House Christmas Party, 1951.

Two years later, the mood was still nostalgic: "But for all the cheer that spread long and wide throughout the large dining room, there were tear-glazed eyes when Dottie Dillard and Bob Johnstone sang Silent Night, Holy Night in soft harmony."[61] The event ended with dancing as the ladies and their dates took to the dance floor. A *Nashville Banner* article captured one special moment in 1951, "To wind up the affair in a truly appropriate fashion, Mrs. Lena Trabue [in her eighties], who was presented to society at the Maxwell House when she was just 18, danced a waltz with Jim Warren of WMAK just to prove that 'once a debutante, always a debutante.'"[62]

After 1958 the location of the Christmas party returned to the Old Woman's Home on West End Avenue. One reason for the relocation was the loss of Maxwell House in a fire in 1961 that destroyed the building, but also likely because new Board officers sought to return to the original mission of the Old Woman's Home—to focus on the care of seniors in Nashville rather than providing an event for the city's social scene. While the event still featured "dates," special prizes, gifts, and entertainment, the OWH holiday celebration was pared down, once again returning to an elaborate dinner "fit for a king" as it had been in the 1920s.

The Golden Girls
Continuity and Change

> For the home is not a charitable institution but a combination of the resources of many old ladies who choose to pool what is left of their fortunes so that they may live comfortably and independently together the rest of their days.
> —*Nashville Tennessean, 1958*

> There are deep emotional ties to the story of the West End Home Foundation—on a human level and as a citizen of Nashville. The good that this organization has done for so many years, in a quiet way, remains phenomenal. The opportunity to serve others is a lesson in grace and gratitude. We must seize it as did our predecessors.
> —*N. Courtney Hollins, Board member 2011–present*

At an event celebrating the fiftieth anniversary of the West End Avenue residence in 1958, Mrs. John F. Hunt (then President of Board of Directors) told those attending: "The home was founded to provide women 65 years or more with a comfortable home, peace of mind, and a feeling of security. And we are still trying to do the same thing. The residents are free to come and go much as in their own homes."[1] And come and go they did. As West End Avenue auto traffic increased in the 1960s and 1970s, many feared that the ladies' habit of darting across West End for a bit of shopping and ice cream was perhaps the "biggest hazard to their health." When a board member asked one of the ladies how she managed to thread her way through

Group dinner, Old Woman's Home, c. 1958.

the heavy traffic, she answered confidently, "Oh, I just shut my eyes and walk straight across."[2]

The OWH moved out to West End Avenue long before early suburban sprawl brought, quite literally, increased traffic and business to their doorstep. Nashville's population and commercial development continued to expand after World War II, and the city's growth spread west. Suddenly, the Old Woman's Home found itself in the middle of a densely commercial area, and as property values skyrocketed and admissions to the home declined, the Board of Directors would make important decisions in the 1970s and 1980s that would usher in a new phase for the charitable corporation. These decisions emphasized continuity of care and reaffirmed the organization's mission, but also recognized the need for change in order to maintain long-term viability.

Loula May Bell, resident and pianist, 1960.

Residents light dinner candles
for special event,1958.

A New Vision for the Aged

The end of the decade that "liked Ike" also signaled the end of an era. The
late 1950s through the 1980s was a period of fluctuation—one that reflected both continuity and change. In 1965 the passage of Medicare, as part of
President Lyndon Johnson's domestic "Great Society" agenda, would extend
health insurance and cover most medical-related costs for individuals over
sixty-five. Not since the passage of the Social Security Act, during Franklin
D. Roosevelt's administration, had senior citizens so greatly benefited from
federal legislation. With the implementation of both Social Security and
Medicare in less than thirty years—the formula for and concept of old age in
America was forever changed.

As a result, the trajectory of how to save, plan, and budget for life after
retirement and the options available to seniors shifted dramatically from
1960 to 1980. The elder care market changed as the modern-day nursing home, a private institution providing residential accommodations with
healthcare for older adults, was born. Between 1960 and 1976 the num-

ber of nursing homes grew by 140 percent. Moreover, during these years the number of beds in nursing homes increased 302 percent, and the privatization of the industry's revenues rose 2,000 percent.[3] In 1971 the Office of Nursing Home Affairs was established, and in 1972, reforms to

Favorite Hobbies Displayed, *Nashville Banner*, c. 1950.

Social Security "established a single set of requirements for facilities supported by Medicare."[4]

In addition to affordable senior healthcare through Medicare, the legal recognition and regulation of charities and volunteer organizations also changed. According to historian Peter Dobkin Hall, the concept of nonprofit enterprises began to take shape in the late 1960s, and the new nonprofit domain provided tax incentives primarily through tax deductions for donors, and the ability to apply for and receive government grants. Additionally, the Tax Reform Act of 1969 introduced sweeping reforms to the charitable sector and included the "first explicit definition of a private foundation as a charitable organization" and defined public charities eligible for tax exemption as organizations related to religious, charitable, scientific, literary, or educational causes.[5] Hall explained the implications of this key shift from charity or foundation to nonprofit as related to health and elder care:

> Industries like healthcare, which had been almost entirely for-profit in ownership before 1950, became dominated by nonprofit firms in the course of the next-half century. On the other hand, industries like elder care, which had been largely nonprofit actually saw an increase in for-profit ownership

as government social and medical insurance programs made nursing homes an increasingly profitable enterprise.[6]

The Old Woman's Home, legally recognized as a charitable corporation since its original charter in 1891, had long served as an institutional model for what would become the nonprofit sector. While the legal status of many charitable and volunteer organizations remained murky until after 1970, the OWH clearly restated its purpose as early as 1946: "The general welfare of society and not individual profit is the object for which the charter was granted, and members are not stockholders and no dividends or profits shall be divided among the members."[7] Official nonprofit status was granted to the organization after the passage of the Tennessee Nonprofit Corporation Act in 1987.[8]

Raising the admission fee in 1956 to $3,000 for all incoming residents, the changes set in motion by Medicare, the expansion of Social Security, and the legal recognition and benefits of nonprofits would ultimately lead to a decline in the number of applicants to the OWH. Residents were still required, as they had been since 1891, to transfer all personal assets to the home including the sale of property, checking, savings, and other individual investments. The types and number of "old ladies…[seeking] to live comfortably and independently together the rest of their days" at the Old Woman's Home would decrease as female senior citizens explored a wider range of retirement living options that did not require them to bequeath their estates to a single institution in return for end-of-life care.[9]

The home had long maintained extensive procedures and vetting for admission. The process began with an application submitted to the home's manager (formerly matron or superintendent). The manager processed all applications, determined which should be advanced, and presented selected applications to the Board of Directors. Following Board approval, each applicant was visited by two staff members at their home and the OWH's head nurse interviewed each lady to assess their "compatibility," according to Anne Gambill Coleman, President of the Board of Directors 1995–1996. Coleman continued, "They had to be friendly, not have any prejudices, and be genuinely excited in coming to the home. This is how it had been for years. Most of those accepted were family friends or had a connection to someone on the Board or Auxiliary."[10] While some came into the home with very little, most had moderate assets, which they turned over in exchange for their care.

Leadership and the Board of Directors

For the first half of the twentieth century, Lizzie Keith and her daughter-in-law Emmy Keith led the OWH Board of Directors as successive Presidents. After Lale L. Murrey's five-year term as Board President (1946–1951), Elizabeth Estes Kirkman was elected to lead the organization. With Kirkman's endorsement, the Board of Directors amended the constitution to elect Board Presidents to a one-year appointment with the possibility of reelection for a second year. Most Presidents served on the board for many years prior to their election as an officer and remained on the Board of Directors after their term. In 1958, the number of Vice-Presidents was permanently set at three, and the Secretary and Treasurer positions rounded out the Board's leadership. The Secretary and Treasurer positions were reelected each year but were not term limited. The number of Board members was increased to twenty-five in 1958.[11] Even though some amendments and revisions were added to the OWH Constitution and Bylaws, the Board's meeting agenda was unchanged from 1958 to 2002. Each meeting opened with a prayer followed by roll call, the reading of the previous meeting's minutes, the Treasurer's report, committee reports, and discussion of unfinished and new business. To all intents and purposes, this meeting agenda remains largely intact today.

However, Old Woman's Home did evolve on an organizational level from 1958 to 1988. For example, the committees in the late 1950s were as follows:

1. Admissions
2. Executive
3. Finance
4. Garden
5. Hospital
6. House
7. Maintenance
8. Endowment and Fundraising
9. Nominating and Constitution
10. Orientation
11. Publicity
12. Purchasing
13. Religious Service
14. Home Visits[12]

Over the course of thirty years, the Board of Directors drastically reduced the number of committees in order to achieve greater efficiency and to streamline the organization's bureaucratic structure. By 1990 standing committees were reorganized into the following groups:

1. Admissions
2. Finance
3. House and Grounds
4. Endowment and Fundraising
5. Nominating and Constitution
6. Health Care Center[13]

Charles R. Clements and men of the Advisory Board dine
with residents of the Old Woman's Home, 1950.

During this time, the OWH leadership also experienced changes. Specifically, the post–World War II era witnessed the death of several individuals important to the OWH's success and reputation. These were stalwart individuals of the community, involved not only in the OWH but also in other community organizations. One such loss was Lillie Morrow Anderson, widow of Judge John McFerrin Anderson, who served as Secretary and Vice-President of the Old Woman's Home in the 1940s and 1950s before her death on February 19, 1957.[14] She was a member of the Colonial Dames and Centennial Club among other local societies.

Longtime Advisory Board member Charles R. Clements passed away on June 1, 1960. Clements was one of the "triumvirate whose efforts enabled National Life to bear the motto 'We Shield Millions,'" where he served as the Vice-President, President, and finally as Board chair.[15] National Life's motto, abbreviated WSM, became the call name for a new radio station sponsored by the insurance company. WSM radio would host a "barn dance" in 1925, which became the famed Grand Ole Opry. Clements was one of the Advisory's Board members who helped to wisely steer the OWH's investments from the late 1930s to the early 1950s. In addition to his careful guidance of the budget and endowment of the Old Woman's Home, Clements was a leading member of the Chamber of Commerce, Board of Governors, and Boards of Trust for Peabody College, Vanderbilt University Hospital, and many other local institutions.

In 1966 another key player in the life of the OWH passed away. Lillian Scott Neel's career included positions as the matron of Founder's Hall, a women's dormitory at Belmont College; the housemother at the Delta Delta Delta sorority house at Vanderbilt University; and finally the residential superintendent of the Old Women's Home.[16]

Six years later, in April 1973, Emmy Keith Jackson died, closing a family chapter of leadership with the Old Woman's Home that had lasted eighty years. A native Nashvillian, Jackson was the granddaughter of Elizabeth Keith and daughter of Walter and Emmy Ewing Keith.[17] Jackson was a charter member of the Junior League of Nashville and a Board member of the Old Women's Home, Ladies Hermitage Association, Polk Memorial Association, and Colonial Dames. (However, at the end of the twentieth century a new leader would emerge from the Keith family tree.) Emmie Jackson McDonald (Board president 1997–1998) is the great-granddaughter of Samuel Jackson and Elizabeth Keith; granddaughter of Walter and Emmy Keith, and daughter of Mr. and Mrs. Robert F. Jackson.[18]

In 1975 Board and Auxiliary member Helen Louise Pickslay Cheek passed away. The family directed contributions to the Old Woman's Home in lieu of flowers.[19] The Cheek family was most famous as part of the Cheek-Neal Company that produced Maxwell House coffee. Cheekwood, the family's fifty-five-acre estate in West Nashville was completed in 1932, and was originally the home of Leslie and Mabel Cheek. Cheekwood was converted into a museum of art and botanical garden in 1960. The Cheek family had donated generously to the OWH throughout the twentieth century, including a large donation to the Auxiliary's nursing fund.[20]

The death of Hortense Bigelow Ingram in 1979 also marked the end of an era. Ingram, widow of O. H. Ingram, former president of Ingram Industries, took seriously her role as a civic leader in Nashville. In addition to serving many years as Treasurer of the Old Woman's Home Board of Directors, she was named a trustee-for-life of the Junior League of Nashville and served on the boards of the Cumberland Museum, Cheekwood, and the Nashville Symphony Association, and helped to found the Ensworth School and Harpeth Hall School.[21] Her daughter, Patricia Ingram Hart, recalls Hortense Bigelow Ingram's attention to detail and dedication to the OWH:

> Mother was a genius with numbers. Every Sunday afternoon she went to the home and answered any resident concerns or questions related to money. She also wrote them a weekly check as a spending allowance. The ladies looked forward to her visits; she loved them and they loved her. She always had their best interests at heart. When my mother died in 1979, they asked me to take her place. But no one could ever take her place, she was so unbelievably smart and passionate about taking care of the elderly.[22]

Two other prominent and longtime advocates passed away in the early 1980s just before the Old Woman's Home became the West End Home for Ladies and moved into the new facility in 1984. Margaret Warner White, daughter of Percy and Margaret Lindsley Warner, passed away on October 20, 1981. White served as member and officer of the OWH Board of Directors for many years; her community involvement also included the Junior League of Nashville, Centennial Club, Ladies Hermitage Association, Colonial Dames, and Historic Belmont Association.[23] Margaret Warner White was part of one of the city's founding families with deep ties to the Nashville Parks Board and Nashville Railway and Light Company (today's NES).

The loss of these individuals, as well as other key supporters, signaled the end of one era and the beginning of another. With determination and resolve, new Board members looked to the future with a renewed sense of purpose. Many Board members extended the organization's multigenerational ties to influential families in Nashville. Such members included Mary Hall "Chippy" Pirtle, Gayle Elam Smith, Emmie Jackson McDonald, Gayle Deerborn Vance, Gray Oliver Thornburg, Jean Ward Oldfield, and Patricia Ingram Hart. Others, such as Carole Minton Nelson, Emily Thompson James, Patricia Kirkman Colton, Bettye Sue Parrish McNeilly, and Jean Dobson Farris were invited to join the Board not only because of their deep community connections but also because of their expertise in finance, investing, elder care, nonprofit management, and civic engagement.

The Board that emerged in the 1980s and 1990s would be responsible for the employment and management of the home and its staff, the organization's mission and resident applications, and the direction of financial resources. These monumental tasks would be more important than ever in a changing market, and the Board of Directors worked proactively to turn such challenges into opportunity.

Evolving Role of the Auxiliary

What began as the Young Women's Auxiliary in 1893 continued, but the group's name was shortened to the "Auxiliary" in the late 1950s. The name change was an effort to modernize and expand membership, but also likely to remove labels associated with age. It was both an honor and a commitment to serve on the Auxiliary, charged by the Board in 1958 to "supply comfort and happiness for the ladies in the home."[24] Based on nominations by existing members, influential women in Nashville were invited to join the group. Nominees also demonstrated their willingness to serve and an interest in the home and its residents. In the 1950s and 1960s membership swelled to nearly seventy members. Governed by its own bylaws and officers, the Auxiliary continued to provide funding for nurses' salaries through a separate budget. After 1960, the Auxiliary phased out their pantry and linen parties, which were charitable drives designed to collect canned goods or gently used sheets, towels, and so on. Public fundraising, sponsored and managed by the Auxiliary, also ended in the early 1960s.

During this era, two important figures connected to the Auxiliary passed away. Mabel Lyon, a civic leader and former president of the Auxiliary, died on May 30, 1956. She was also active in the following organizations: Colonial Dames,

Mabel Lyon, a longtime supporter of the Old Woman's Home and local civic leader passed away in 1956.

Centennial Club, Belle Meade Country Club, Peabody Aid, Vanderbilt Aid, Kipling Club, and the Nashville Press and Authors Club.[25] Nine years later, Anita Lewis Frazer died at the age of eighty-one. Frazer was the first vice president of the women's suffrage movement in Nashville and served as president of the Young Women's Auxiliary in the 1940s. Her father, Eugene Castner Lewis, was the chairman of the Centennial Exposition of 1897 and architect of the Parthenon and Union Station. When she married James Stokes Frazer, she married into an extended family that had long supported the OWH through volunteerism and donations.[26]

By the 1980s, membership in the Auxiliary was approximately forty women. The group's size was not diminished because of any mandate or rule change but rather more practical reasons: fewer residents, less fundraising responsibility, and the hiring of more full-time staff that included an executive director (formerly matron or superintendent) and activities director.

From its inception, the Auxiliary focused on ways in which they could support the residents in their daily lives. In 1924 the *Nashville Banner* reported: "The Old

Two residents play cards after dinner.

Woman's Home Auxiliary decided that more visits should be paid at the home and all try to get in a personal touch with the inmates. Every month a godmother was selected for each of the old ladies, and it was expected that special attention should be given to her during the month."[27] This tradition continued through the years as the Auxiliary focused less on raising money and more on providing companionship for the ladies of the OWH.

In the 1970s the Auxiliary members traded in the system of selecting "godmothers" in favor of adopted "buddies." The "buddy" system became the Auxiliary's most important function, one that brought much joy to the residents. Auxiliary members rotated in taking residents shopping and on outings such as trips to the movies, concerts at the Nashville Symphony, and events at the Tennessee Performing Arts Center, War Memorial Auditorium, and other venues.[28] In the 1980s, Auxiliary members often took their buddy out for a lunch date and an afternoon activity. A typical outing might include lunch at the Picnic Café near St. Thomas Hospital West, a trip to the Castner Knott or the French Shoppe in Green Hills, and a manicure at Nails Exclusively by Salt and Pepper on West End Avenue.[29]

As always, holidays and birthdays remained monumental events in the home, and parties were largely planned and hosted by Auxiliary members. The Auxiliary stuffed Christmas stockings, filled Easter baskets, organized weekly bingo games, and hosted monthly birthday celebrations. The Auxiliary was in close contact with the ever-popular and energetic Rita Lush, who served as activities director at the home from 1999 to 2005, and Claire Weneberger, longtime superintendent-turned-executive director of the Old Woman's Home.

Residents in front of the West End Avenue facility before an outing with Auxiliary members, c. 1975. First row: Eleanor Hix, Theresa Shockley, Imelda Hughes, Ruby Bowles, Charity Comingore; Second row: Wynona Rauscher, Gertrude Jones; Third row: Katie Lou Gatlin, Lucille Mullendore, Ruth Holliday; Fourth row: Aneska Massey, Frances Morrissey, Hilda Owen, May Bransford, Lucille Massey; Fifth row: Ada Stephenson, Clara Feldhaus, Louise White, Martha Cook.

The Auxiliary also took advantage of special events in the local area. Cemele Richardson, a dedicated Auxiliary member and officer, recalled the coordination between the Auxiliary and staff to take the ladies for a tethered hot air balloon ride at Percy Warner Park, after which news coverage made it the "talk of the town."[30] The event was part of the Music City Hot Air Balloon Festival which took place in the 1980s near the open field used for the Iroquois Steeplechase. For many outings the ladies would "dress to the nines," and this time was no different. In heels and pearls, residents enjoyed the ride as well as the food and festivities on the ground. In 2015, the annual festival was revived as reported by the *Tennessean*, "At dusk Saturday, West Nashville's sky will light up with giant, glowing, colorful balloons. A tradition decades ago, the Music City Hot Air Balloon Festival returns to Percy Warner Park."[31]

Clare Weneberger and residents celebrate with dress hats, 1989. Front row: Bettye Moore, Belle Austin; Second row: Lucille Massey, Virginia Collins, Myrtle Trotter, Lucy Mullendore, Ann Arnett, Katie Gatlin; Third row: Mildred Anderson, Claire Weneberger, Oda Stephenson.

Regardless of the activity or event, the caring relationship between the Auxiliary and the residents was undeniable. Auxiliary member Phyllis Heard commented that "what the ladies like best of all is a visit from members of the Auxiliary."[32] Edith Miller, who joined the Auxiliary in the early 1990s, said she loved the home because "we [Auxiliary] paid so much attention to them [ladies]."[33] Many in the Auxiliary acted as surrogate daughters to their "buddy" and were "very close."[34] As is often the case with volunteer opportunities, Auxiliary members found that they received as much joy, if not more, than they gave.

A New Name, A New Home

The Old Woman's Home on West End Avenue stood as a local landmark and passersby were accustomed to seeing the ladies on the porch and around the neighborhood. In the 1960s the OWH welcomed Vanderbilt fraternity pledges who came to wash the home's windows every year for over a decade. The *Tennessean* captured one such moment: "Members of Vanderbilt chapter of Kappa Sigma fraternity take down screens and wash windows at the old women's home. A fraternity spokesman said the work day is a substitution for what was once 'Hell Week.'"[35] A few of the ladies chatted with the young men from their windows while they

Vanderbilt University pledges from Sigma Alpha Epsilon wash windows during "Help Week" substituted for "Hell Week" during the fall fraternity rush season. Pledges include Gene Joyce, Don Hunt, Roy Keathley, and Pete Nebhut (left to right), 1961.

cleaned—which perhaps conjured memories of serenades and male suitors from a by-gone era. When the job was finished, the residents and the "boys" visited together and shared drinks, food, and stories.

The residents and staff at the home formed an extended family with close bonds, but even so, there could also be moments of stress and anxiety in a peaceful and serene place to reside. One particularly frightening incident was

on Sunday, November 26, 1961, when the Nashville Fire Department rushed two ladder trucks and three engines to the OWH to put out a small blaze. The fire was caused by a rag left inadvertently in a pot of boiling water. As a local newspaper reported: "When the water

Youth group performance, 1971.

boiled away the rag caught fire."[36] Fortunately, the fire was put out with minimal damage and no injuries were reported.

After decades of debate about the name of the home, the Board of Directors made the difficult decision. In 1981 the beloved but bluntly named Old Woman's Home was renamed the West End Home for Ladies. The first attempt to change the name first surfaced in the 1920s when the Board initially passed a motion to adopt the name "Elizabeth Home" or "Elizabeth House" in honor of Lizzie Keith—but the resolution was never implemented. In the 1950s, conversation surfaced once again as some Board members sought to modernize the organization's designated title. In the 1970s another short-lived campaign to change the name to Magnolia Hall failed to gain traction. While there were these periodic efforts to rename the organization, the Old Woman's Home remained the Old Woman's Home for ninety years.

Several factors contributed to the name's endurance. Legally the institution's state charter of incorporation stated that the founders "constituted a body politic and corporation by the name and style of the Old Woman's Home."[37] Another legality that kept the OWH-brand intact was the nature of the home's greatest source of funding—donations made through bequests. Many in leadership over the years feared that changing the charitable corporation's name would create a loophole for families to contest the gift of the deceased relative.

Through the 1980s, the Auxiliary and residents enjoyed formal teas.

In addition to legal reasons, the Old Woman's Home was widely recognized as one of Nashville's worthiest causes. As such, the OWH sought to maintain the culture of trust and respect with the local community, which had been cultivated over many decades. And what did the "old women" in the "Old Woman's Home" think about the name change? Many of the forty residents living in the home in 1981 objected. However, the Old Woman's Home increasingly sounded antiquated and even condescending to the broader community, and the Board of Directors made the decision to move forward as the West End Home for Ladies (WEHFL).

The newly minted West End Home for Ladies represented the first step in an organizational reset, so to speak. With its new name, the WEHFL indicated the type of women it sought to attract—middle- to upper-class white women with a history of work, family connections, and/or community leadership. The second step in the effort to reset was the sale of the Victorian home on West End and the move to a new facility on Vanderbilt Place. This represented a literal move to downsize while remaining culturally relevant and financially viable.

Though the Victorian on West End Avenue had been meticulously maintained, the seventy-five-year-old structure was showing its age. The home still lacked private bathrooms and central heating and air-conditioning, and the electrical and plumbing systems were original to the building and needed replacement. Some took matters into their own hands. Several residents upgraded from ceiling fans in their rooms to electric air-conditioning window units while at least one resident had a private sink installed in her room.[38]

Two years after the charter was amended to change the organization's name to the West End Home for Ladies, the Board of Directors faced another stark choice: make massive renovations to the Victorian residence or sell and build on a lot behind the property. Additionally, federal health laws and

The kitchen in the West End Avenue facility, 1983.

state/local regulations to bring the buildings up to code made renovations costs so high that new construction emerged as the most viable option. Betty Sue Parrish McNeilly, former Board member and daughter-in-law of Corinne Parrish (Board of Directors President from 1981 to 1983), summed up the events that led to the ultimate decision to relocate: "Ted Welch and the Spiva Hill Management wanted to develop the property on West End Avenue, and we needed a new home."[39]

Randall Yearwood was selected as the architect for the new building, and Board President Chippy Pirtle (1979–1981) was also instrumental in the planning, negotiations, and construction. The new facility was built as a grand colonial with four Doric white pillars. Board members Betty Sue Parrish McNeilly and Patricia Ingram Hart worked closely with the architect on the design.[40] A Board member for over thirty years, Hart explained the thought process of the building committee as they finalized construction plans: "We wanted Vanderbilt Place to match the style of other buildings on the street, and we also felt it

Employees, staff, and board members, 1982.

was important for it to look and feel like a home. Those factors led us to choose a classic colonial style."[41]

According to legal documents executed, the developers agreed to complete the construction of the new facility before tearing down the old West End Home for Ladies' complex. The arrangement was a good compromise

Construction of the new facility at 2818 Vanderbilt Place.

for all involved despite the sadness many felt surrounding the impending demolition of the West End Avenue complex. While the decision was bittersweet, it remained timely as the condition of the home grew more noticeable.

The decision to move was not without motivating financial interests related to the property value of the 2.59 acres on West End Avenue. The original lot was quite large, so it was possible to subdivide the lot. The OWH retained the back quarter of the lot in exchange for the portion of the lot facing West End Avenue. The developers then absorbed the costs of the new home's construction, which would face Vanderbilt Place, a side street running parallel to West End Avenue. The unique transactional arrangement between the OWH and Spiva Hill developers was recorded by Jay Grannis, the organization's accountant, in the annual financial statement: "The land and building, which is carried at fair market value was arrived at based on the exchange value of the new building at a cost of $1.7 million for the old building and land ($306,000)."[42]

The move from 2817 West End Avenue to 2818 Vanderbilt Place in

Laying the new cornerstone at 2818 Vanderbilt Place.

Completed facility at 2818 Vanderbilt Place, 1985.

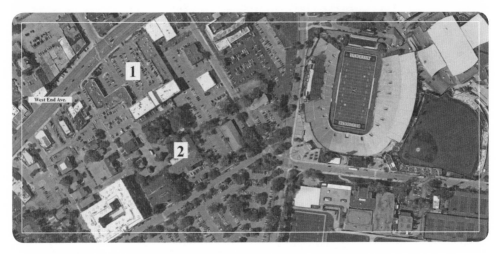

Aerial view of West End property and Vanderbilt Place facility.

1984 did not require a carriage ride, as had the last move from downtown in 1909, but rather a walk through the backyard garden. The dedication and opening of the new home took place on June 3, 1984, a warm day in Nashville with temperatures over 90 degrees. The heat did not keep a large crowd from gathering for the home's grand opening. With over 220 people in attendance, guests enjoyed a reception and toured the facility that included forty residential rooms, each with a full bathroom. The WEHFL also had private phone lines installed in each room. The building featured a three-story open foyer and reception area, offices, an elevator, large dining room, living room on each floor, beauty parlor, and a guest suite for visiting family and friends. In addition, all rooms were single occupancy, which allowed more room for personal furniture and keepsakes. This was in stark contrast to the Victorian home, completed in 1909. As Hart recalled, "The old home was dark with heavy furniture and drapes, and we wanted the new building to be open, fresh, and modern."[43]

Despite the modern amenities, Nettie Jane Langhans, past President of the Auxiliary, recalled that some of the ladies missed the West End home and did not like the Vanderbilt Place home at first. According to Langhans, "It was so different and felt institutional compared to the West End facility. Vanderbilt Place faced a parking lot...and did not have the grand spaces

Two attendees at new home's grand opening, 1984.

and views" of the old verandas, which looked out on West End Avenue.[44] However, it took little time for the ladies to appreciate private rooms, bathrooms, phones, and air-conditioning. Within a few months, the residents and staff looked back at the West End home with fondness rather than sadness and settled into a familiar routine—but with the ladies gladly riding in the new elevator.

Life at Vanderbilt Place

Life at Vanderbilt Place for residents continued much as it had on West End Avenue. Half of the residents had never married and the other half were widows. Some had never been part of the paid labor force but rather chose to do

Louise Hobbs and Muriel C. King.

volunteer work. However, many of the home's women had worked as professionals—teachers, nurses, secretaries, and even small business owners. Examples include Wilma Short, a nurse at St. Thomas hospital; Mary Elizabeth Allen, a retired teacher whose tenure included twenty-six-years at Caldwell Elementary School; Muriel King, a longtime employee at National Life and Accident Insurance Company; and Louise Gatlin Hobbs, who worked for Life and Casualty Insurance Company.[45] (These two insurance companies merged in the 1980s after the retirement of Hobbs and King.)

As had been the tradition, prior to moving in, residents signed contracts pledging to abide by the home's rules, which included no arguing and no cook-

Fountain and benches at Vanderbilt Place facility, 1989.

ing or hot plates in rooms. Additionally, the ladies were asked to "dress for dinner." The home's tenants entertained guests; embroidered, knitted, and sewed; and showed off their collective green thumb with "front porch gardens" and potted plants. Although the backyard at Vanderbilt Place was significantly smaller than the original West End property, the flower and shrub-filled garden flanked a tranquil patio and fountain. Some ladies like to cut and trim flowers, and they often sat on benches around the large water fountain, moved from the old property, to chat when the weather permitted.

Despite efforts to create community and congeniality, tensions between some residents sometimes existed. Anne Gambill Coleman recalled that not all residents were a good fit for the home and for the rest of the group: "One lady was asked to move after the home's staff agreed as she was giving the infirmary a hard time."[46] Janie Macey, an Auxiliary member in the 1980s and 1990s, recalled that her "buddy" Marie Pike, called "Mouse" because she was so tiny, also endured some difficult moments at the WEHFL: "Most wom-

en were of the upper echelon but Marie Pike was not. But Marie was feisty and did not let it bother her. It made me love her even more."[47] Former Board member Patricia Ingram Hart perhaps summed it up best: "They were just like any other group of ladies; they were all smart and opinionated. The home was a happy place, but some of the residents raised trouble from time to time."[48]

One thing that united all of the ladies was music. Sarah McConnell began volunteering at the home in 1989

Marie Pike at local Nashville
Fire Station, 2009.

after meeting her neighbor, Claire Weneberger, the home's director in the 1980s and early 1990s. McConnell recalled, "I'd start playing the guitar or dulcimer, and the ladies would call out requests and often joined me in singing."[49] They looked forward to her visits and their sing-a-long favorites included "Let Me Call You Sweetheart," "Tea for Two," "In the Garden" and "The Prisoner's Song." McConnell later founded the nonprofit organization Music for Seniors, in part because of her experiences at the home. "One of the lovely things about going to the West End Home for Ladies was meeting the ladies, talking to them, hearing their stories, and connecting with them," she said.[50]

Previously referred to as the infirmary or hospital wing in the old home, the new facility included the West End Health Care Center that was equipped with thirteen beds, medical equipment, and nurses on duty twenty-four hours a day. Doctors came to the West End Health Care Center for doctor's visits and emergencies, so the ladies rarely traveled to a doctor's office or hospital. Dr. Robert Quinn served as the primary physician for West End Home for Ladies and regularly made house calls for check-ups, tests, illness, or injury. The healthcare staff also included beloved nurses such as Sue Duncan, Gina Johnson, Terronda Henderson, and Frances Ducrest. Anne Gambill Coleman, President of the Board of Directors (1995–1996), validated the important role of the staff: "Nurses were very helpful in the psychological assessment and chemistry of applicants and residents."[51]

The Board and Auxiliary depended heavily on the staff, who served officially as caretakers but also played important but unofficial roles as counselors, companions, and intermediaries between the residents and leadership. Great care was taken in filling staff positions, and most devoted their professional careers to the home and its residents. As Emmie McDonald, Board President (1997–1998) concluded: "The home had wonderful and qualified staff in every area. They were excellent, long-term, active, and made the ladies happy."[52]

Dining room at Vanderbilt Place with Teresa Jones (left)
and the home's director Randy Cornwell (center).

The way to a man's heart is through his stomach, the old adage goes, but as it turns out, it is also the way to a *woman's* heart. Daily highlights at the WEHFL centered around the meals provided by the home. The head chef, Teresa Jones, dedicated her talents to the West End Home for Ladies for more than fifteen years. Gayle Vance recalled one of Teresa's greatest acts of love: "If she knew that one of the residents was not eating well or was sick, Teresa would make her favorite foods. Teresa knew what they all liked best and made sure they had it. Simply put—she was amazing."[53]

In addition to Teresa's leadership behind the scenes, Nettie Jane Langhans stated, "The entire kitchen staff was wonderful, and they were great cooks."[54] Her grandmother, Hilda Owens, was a resident and Langhans often visited the home to have lunch with her grandmother. Several members of the Auxiliary recalled the delicious home cooking prepared and served by a kitchen staff "who really loved the ladies."[55] Particularly noteworthy was Thursday, known as Fried Chicken Day. Sarah McConnell concurred, "The West End

Home for Ladies had the best food in Nashville. Lunch at the home was a real treat—the food, the beautiful big dining room with white tablecloths, and of course the ladies."[56]

While in the 1990s the residents no longer wore white gloves and pearls for formal dinners or teas, most continued to wear dinner attire that included dresses, hosiery, and jewelry. After dinner, ladies retired to the common living room, where they played canasta or checkers and watched television. *Jeopardy* (which first aired in 1964) and *Wheel of Fortune* (which premiered in 1975) could be heard coming from the common rooms, and the ladies never tired of answering in the form of a question or solving the puzzle.[57]

Residents also ventured out to restaurants two or three times a month. These culinary field trips began in the 1980s when one of the residents discovered a column in the *Tennessean* called "Out of the Way Gourmet," featuring restaurants throughout Middle Tennessee. Soon the ladies were checking out the cuisine at Pearl's Restaurant in Sewanee, Foglight Foodhouse near Center Hill Lake, Miss Bobo's in Lynchburg, and the High Point restaurant in Monteagle. These outings were

Group from the West End Home for Ladies enjoy the General Jackson dinner and riverboat cruise.

organized by Claire Weneberger, the Director of the home in the 1980s and 1990s. Weneberger was loved by all connected to the home, and her passion for senior care and the relationship with the ladies was evident. She planned trips to see performances by the Rockettes and the play *Phantom of the Opera* in Nashville, as well as visits to Montgomery Bell State Park and the Amish Village near Munfordville, Kentucky.

Some traditions stood the test of time such as tea parties, birthdays, Bible studies, and holiday celebrations. During Christmas season, Auxiliary members presented each of their "buddies" with a stocking, carolers from local churches and schools visited, and festive decorations adorned the tree and home. There were also new favorites at Vanderbilt Place that reflected changing times. Movies like *Steel*

Group photo in new living room of Vanderbilt Place facility with watercolor painting of the West End Avenue facility over the mantle, 1984.

Magnolias, Home Alone, The Princess Bride, An Officer and a Gentleman, Fried Green Tomatoes, and of course, *Driving Miss Daisy* were shown in the healthcare wing sunroom.

Perhaps the favorite new activity for residents in the 1980s and 1990s was weekly bingo. As Grace Smith Bathrick, active and longtime member of the Auxiliary, recalled: "Bingo was a big deal at the Vanderbilt Place home. Alfred (maintenance) set up the tables and chairs…Each bingo night, volunteer members brought five prizes, one for each of the four games and one for a tie."[58] Woody Richardson, Cemele Richardson's husband, and other Auxiliary members called the bingo games each week.

One particular resident who loved bingo was Bettye Moore, who was admitted to the home in 1989. Bathrick said Mrs. Moore "was so cute" at only five feet tall.[59] Cindy Dickinson added that Bettye helped to set up weekly bingo and "could keep up with three or four cards at once."[60] In

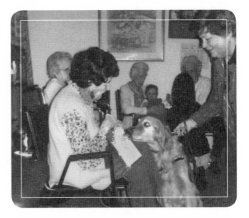

Bettye Moore, Gayle Vance, and Bailey the dog.

addition to her enthusiasm for games, Mrs. Moore participated in every Bible study and was usually the first to arrive. She also enjoyed reading, making flower arrangements, crossword and jigsaw puzzles, music programs, arts and crafts, traveling, and was known for her trademark "fancy, large earrings."[61] In the *West End Home for Ladies Newsletter*, Mrs. Moore spoke to the importance of community and connection: "Nashville is my home and returning here with the members of my family still living has been wonderful for me. I believe God has led me to the place he knew I should be."[62] Bettye Moore was only one of many residents who appreciated and contributed to the quality of life at the West End Home for Ladies.

Toward the New Millennium

The West End Home for Ladies continued to model the importance of community and senior care; the organization also celebrated a century of service in 1991. But despite the unparalleled care provided and a new name and facility, changes set in motion by government programs and the rise of for-profit homes and in-home care services led to a decline in the number of applicants. By the 1990s, applications had dropped so substantially that only

News article about Charity Stagg Comingore, *Tennessean*, 1983.

Group photo in living room of Vanderbilt Place facility, 1984.

two women were denied admission to the WEHFL between 1990 and 2002. Anne Gambill Coleman stated: "Fewer applied because of Social Security and other things, and [more] women worked and earned an income. In addition, families started thinking, wait a minute—we don't want Grandmother to turn over everything."[63]

There *were* still women who wanted to live out their lives according to the West End Home for Ladies model. In fact, more than sixty women entered the home after the move to the new building in 1983; however, many of them had no living children. One such example was Charity Stagg Comingore, who worked as the administrative assistant to the President of Berea College for over twenty years before moving to Nashville to work at Peabody College for Teachers. After admission to the WEHFL, Miss Comingore's local fame for recipes and culinary talents culminated in a cookbook entitled *Tea with Charity* (see article page 88).

Ladies at Vanderbilt Place relax in common living area upstairs, 1989.

Another such example was Josephine "Jo" Sweeney. Mrs. Sweeney's father owned a coal mine in Kentucky, and she attended Georgetown College and later Western Kentucky Teachers College. After completing coursework, Mrs. Sweeney taught music before working as a department store buyer and moving with her husband to Nashville.[64] After her retirement from the Cain Sloan Department Store and the death of her husband, Mrs. Sweeney applied for admission to the West End Home for Ladies after encouragement and recommendations from members of her congregation—Woodmont Baptist Church. Sweeney's application was accepted by the Board of Directors, and she entered the home in 1987 at the age of eighty. In addition to her monthly Social Security, her assets, signed over legally to the home, were typical of most residents during this era:

$103,800 sale of home
$88,490 additional property
$28,659 savings account
$2,173 checking account
$5,000 stocks, bonds, and securities
= $228,122 total assets[65]

The continued wise investment of the organization's existing endowment and the estates of residents such as Jo Sweeney, as well as fundraising and investments held by the Auxiliary, put the WEHFL on firm fiduciary footing. However, by 2000 it was apparent that women like Jo Sweeney no longer wanted to transfer legal control of their estates to the home and sought other available living options.

Even so, the WEHFL's endowment and management kept the institution's financial future secure—at least on paper. Carole Minton Nelson served for many years as the Treasurer and a member of the Board of Directors. As part of the Board she also served for decades as a member of the investment committee and finance committee. Nelson's dedicated service would span an incredible thirty-three years (1983–2016). Nelson was joined by Patricia Kirkman Colton. Colton was a sophisticated financier and WEHFL Board member who held multiple positions of leadership in the larger Nashville community. Nelson and Colton were forced to make several bold moves to protect the home's money in the late 1980s and 1990s after the WEHFL's primary bank failed to follow directives about selling and buying certain stocks.

Nelson sought the advice of Bill Spitz, Vanderbilt University's Treasurer, as well as Jay Grannis, the organization's trusted financial advisor and accountant, and moved the home's investments to a new firm—diversifying the overall portfolio. The recession of 1986 placed a great deal of stress on members of the investment committee. As Nelson recalls: "I was so worried about our financial security in the mid-1980s, I couldn't sleep."[66]

Ultimately, Colton and Nelson's perseverance and attentiveness literally paid dividends. The balance of the home's assets grew from $7,143,538 in 1983 to approximately $9,900,000 in 1990 to more than $15,000,000 in 2002 (for more see chapter 4). As Nelson reflected, "I was very proud of all the committee work related to finance and investment during my years at the foundation. We helped the home's investments grow and we fought to stay on top of things—in good times and bad."[67] Gray Oliver Thornburg, who joined the Board in 2002 and served as president from 2012 to 2014, concluded:

> Carole Nelson is one of the most thorough and thoughtful women I have ever had the pleasure to work with on any committee or Board. She was diligent and detail oriented when it came to the finances of the Board, along with Patricia Colton who was an incredibly educated stock manager; I saw Patricia many a morning at Starbucks reading the *Journal* or the *Financial Times*. Carole kept meticulous notes during the quarterly meetings, made detailed reports to the Board monthly, and kept a constant eye on the accounts and results. We would not be where we are today without them.[68]

Despite the financial bottom line, as the new millennium approached, the overall model of retirement living provided by the West End Home for Ladies teetered on uneven ground as public programs and private options expanded. The club-like atmosphere of the WEHFL in the post–World War II era was based on the chemistry and refinement of its residents. If the organization hoped to remain nonprofit, the applicant pool would have to expand beyond "gentle women of birth" (as they had originally been identified a century earlier) to comply with federal and state nondiscrimination laws that governed and regulated human service programs. Such developments would lead the Board of Directors to reimagine the future of the foundation and its fundamental shift from a residential to nonresidential model.

The Legacy Continues
Joining the Past, Present, and Future

" We gather to celebrate our ladies and to remember their lives and ours—as we were intertwined with them. We were their families; they were our friends.
—*Gray Oliver Thornburg, 2014*

" In so many ways, the West End Home Foundation represents a family tradition—multiple generations of women helping women. Our resources today are a result of this tradition. We still have much to offer; we still have many to serve.
—*Gayle Deerborn Vance, 2017*

Jean Ward Oldfield's earliest memory of the Old Woman's Home was in the 1930s: "My grandmother would take me by the hand and we would walk up to the West End home. I remember fondly sisters Maude Payne and Cora Kallock who lived on the first floor in rooms off of the large entry hall." Oldfield did not realize then that she would visit the ladies of the home for the next seventy-plus years as a longtime member of the Auxiliary and Board of Directors. She also reflected on the organization's role in Nashville as a force for good: "The OWH was so successful in the early years in part because it was not competing with other charities." Oldfield added, "It was also the worthiest cause and best managed organization in Nashville, but the last fifty years have brought great change to the worlds of senior care and charities."[1]

Growing up in 1950s Nashville, Gayle Deerborn Vance accompanied her mother as part of a larger group who visited the Old Woman's Home each year to sing Christmas carols. Vance credits the service of her mother as the inspiration for her "commitment of a lifetime." She stated, "My mother passed that love and passion to me. She died a year before I joined the Auxiliary, but I have always felt as though my work with the West End Home Foundation was a way to stay connected to her. It also gave me the opportunity to work to make a positive difference in regard to elder and senior care."[2]

Oldfield, Vance, and many others connected to the West End Home Foundation represent one of the West End Home Foundation's greatest strengths—the multigenerational support of Nashville women committed to the care of Nashville's seniors. The Board of Directors summarized it best:

> Our roots run deep in the Nashville community. For more than 125 years, it has been our privilege to serve as a unique institution dedicated to the care of seniors. Ours is a story of perseverance through changing times. It is a story of people, motivated by compassion, working together to give seniors in need a place to call home, where the anxiety of facing a bleak and uncertain future is replaced by the bonds of love and security.[3]

A New Era of Senior Care

In 1969, William C. Thomas Jr., an expert in public health and professor at Columbia University, described the evolving nature of elder care, "The story of public policy in relation to nursing homes has been one of broadening administrative boundaries to encompass more and more phenomena...This trend may be expected to continue."[4] Writing in the same year, Martin Cherkasky, MD, anticipated a strategic realignment of options for old age based on a system of integrated, comprehensive medical delivery for all stages of life: "Implicit in the new definition of healthcare should be a direct responsibility for the care of the long-term patient."[5] As predicted by Thomas and Cherkasky, this shift in health and residential care for seniors developed over several decades. In addition to a wider range of healthcare and residential options, technology and in-home care would emerge as major factors allowing seniors to remain in their homes. Though the transition was gradual, it became apparent to the Board of Directors that the landscape had shifted.

In 1960, the number of residents at the Old Woman's Home exceeded sixty women. By the 1970s, the number of ladies living at the OWH hovered in the mid forties. From 1980 to 1999, resident applications and admissions continued to dwindle—with only twenty-two residents by 2000. As the new millennium approached, the Board of Directors addressed these and other challenges to the organizational model of the home. Cindy Dickinson noted:

> Times were changing. Many more "retirement homes" were available. Increasingly, seniors were choosing to live independently and stay in their homes. As more and more women entered the workforce and established professional careers, they improved their financial standing and became less dependent on institutions like the West End Home for Ladies.[6]

Jean Dobson Farris, member of the Auxiliary, Board of Directors, and Board President from 2009 to 2011, discussed the effect of market changes, "We had to ask ourselves, are we the right people? Was this the right model to achieve our goals of senior care? We were not healthcare professionals. We hired professionals, and we had an excellent healthcare wing. That said, we were *not* a hospital, and we were *not* a profit-driven business."[7]

By 2000, private nursing homes had become a "$100 billion industry, paid largely by Medicaid, Medicare, and out-of-pocket expenses," according to

Residents and guests visit in the foyer of Vanderbilt Place facility, 2003.

historian Carole Haber.[8] From 2000 to 2015, traditional nursing homes would give way to expanded senior housing options from independent/assisted living to home/memory care—tripling the elder-care market to over $300 billion by 2015. The total number of people over the age of sixty-five also continued to increase in the twenty-first century as did life expectancy for American seniors. The Administration on Aging noted a 28 percent growth from 36.2 million seniors in 2004 to 46.2 million in 2014, with the average woman reaching age sixty-five projected to live an additional twenty years and men age sixty-five projected to live an additional eighteen years.[9] The West End Home Foundation's Executive Board navigated a series of complicated circumstances at the turn of the century as these changes were taking place.

Difficult Decisions

In 2001, eighteen years after the move to Vanderbilt Place, the Board voted to become a private foundation and to legally rename the organization "The West

End Home Foundation." With this change, the WEHF began accepting applications and awarding grants to Middle Tennessee organizations whose services centered on senior care. Simultaneously, the Board also approved a resolution to halt new admissions to the home.

Prior to this decision, some of the last residents to be admitted were Ida Hildred Dingess (1996), Marie Stewart Laurent Fuqua (1997), Shelley Childress Cabell Blitch (1998), Moselle Florence Martin (1998), Annie Rai Doyal Shaw (1998), Rosalyn Critser Smith (1999), Willie Mae Huddleston Stivers (1999), Louise Gatlin Hobbs (1999), Lizzie Burt Dobbs Young Hutchinson (2000), and Charlene LaRue Shirley Bomer (2000).[10] An exception was made for Velma Doss, who was admitted to the home on September 1, 2005. Miss Doss had spent much of her professional life at the home as a beloved nurse who served in the infirmary at the Old Woman's Home on West End Avenue. When the Board of Directors learned that she was in ill health, they unanimously voted to admit her. Tragically, Miss Doss passed away just six weeks later on October 17, 2005. The organization's decision to adopt a new name and transition from residential to nonresidential services was formalized through amendments to the WEHF's constitution and bylaws in 2002.

While these were difficult decisions, in reality they were years in the making. Board members such as Patricia Kirkman Colton, Kathryn Craig Henry, Ruth Rodemyer Weaver, Carole Minton Nelson, and others were instrumental in recognizing changes in the elder care sector in the late 1980s.

Trip to Radnor Lake, 2001.

In the early 1990s, the Board of Directors and the Nashville community lost two great leaders in Ruth Rodemyer Weaver and Kathryn Craig Henry.[11] The *Tennessean* praised Henry as a "Nashville civic leader" after her death in 1990. Henry was the mother of state Senator Douglas Henry Jr. and the daughter of Mr. and Mrs. Cornelius Craig. Her father was one of the founders of the National Life and Accident Insurance Company. Henry was a longtime Board member of the Old Woman's Home, Protestant Orphanage, and Nashville Opera Association, as well as regent of the Ladies Hermitage Association, and founding member of the Junior League of Nashville.[12] Ruth Rodemyer Weaver was also extremely active in Nashville and worked in several capacities for local organizations dedicated to improving conditions for those less fortunate and more vulnerable. She was the president of the Board of Directors for the Old Woman's Home from 1971 to 1973, but was a Board member for many years. She also served on the boards of Vanderbilt Children's Hospital, United Way, Family and Children's Services, Salvation Army, and Ensworth School. She passed away in March 1994, at the age of seventy-two.[13]

New leadership on the Board rose to meet challenges and included Jean Dobson Farris, Gray Oliver Thornburg, Frances Johnston Earthman, Gayle Elam Smith, Mary Herbert Kelly, Emily Thompson James, Drake Thompson Calton, and Gayle Deerborn Vance. Members of the Board in the late 1990s and early 2000s were visionary in identifying and understanding why and how the market had changed. Private nursing homes, assisted living, memory-care, home healthcare, and other transitory facilities all provided services for fees. It grew increasingly clear that the WEHF's model of total asset transference in return for total care was no longer in demand for the types of women that the organization had served for over a century. More broadly these changes reflected the seismic shift of U.S. culture over the course of the twentieth century related to women's autonomy, retirement and aging, and financial planning. As Gayle Vance, former Auxiliary and Board President, noted:

What we had to offer no longer fit the modern senior care land-scape. For so many years we had a waiting list, and suddenly not only did the waiting list disappear but so did the applications. Something was not connecting. We talked to ministers and other nonprofits; we talked to our financial advisers and lawyers; we had to adapt and expand our mission if we were to survive as an organization that supported seniors.[14]

In addition to changing markets and models, there were significant increases in the amount of regulation. New safety and medical regulations, mostly at the state level, made it much more difficult and expensive to run and operate a facility that offered independent living, assisted living, and nursing care all under one roof. In 2003, a sea-changing event occurred that forced the Board to consider what residential option was best for the remaining residents. On September 26 the NHC Healthcare Center, located in downtown Nashville, suffered a horrific fire. The national news lead-in was "Bedridden patients screamed for help and firefighters carried the elderly down ladders and stairs as a fire spread through a four-story nursing home with no sprinkler system [legally exempted], killing eight and critically injuring sixteen."[15] Among those who died was ninety-six-year-old Thelma Connelly remembered as "feisty and sweet," who was also the mother of the District's Fire Chief Bobby Connelly.

The tragedy hit close to home, literally and figuratively, for the WEHF. The Vanderbilt Place building was constructed with a sprinkler system in all common areas: living rooms, dining hall, lobby, and healthcare center. However, there were no sprinklers in the bedrooms. By the time of the NHC fire, the West End home had stopped admissions but had not yet decided whether to move or stay on at the Vanderbilt Place facility. Nashville reacted to the nursing home fire by implementing new regulations, ordinances, and codes over the next several years.

The nine residents who moved to the Blakeford: (back row) Bettye Moore, Shelley Blitch, Rita Lush (staff), Liz Hutchinson, Charlene Bomer, Marie Pike, guest; (front row) Lillian Harley, Culla Keith, Ruth Beaver, (not pictured Eleanor Hersh).

Gayle Vance recalled Board discussions about the impact of the 2003 tragedy and the possibility of the WEHF as a legal assisted living facility: "One of the new requirements for assisted living was the ability of residents to evacuate the building in a fire or emergency (for example ability to get down the stairs) to qualify for assisted living," Vance continued, "I don't know how Mrs. Hersh would have gotten down from the third floor. We knew we would need to do major renovations if the home was to stay open. The nursing home fire was certainly in the back of our minds as we made decisions between 2003 and 2009."[16]

Such challenge and change impacted the West End Home Foundation, but the Board acted with thoughtful deliberation, pragmatism, and vision. As N. Courtney Hollins noted, "The Board of Directors during that period did a brilliant job putting together all the nuts and bolts necessary to make that transition and to create a new sustainable model, while keeping the needs of the residents first."[17]

Growing Pains and Governance

Between 2001 and 2007, storm clouds gathered over issues related to the West End Home Foundation's governance. Many active on the Auxiliary worried about their diminished role within the organization after the Board's decision to stop accepting new residents. By 2007, fewer than fifteen residents remained in the home with more than forty Auxiliary members. Beyond their role as volunteers at the home, they also had a financial interest in the future of the organization since the Auxiliary had been the primary fundraising arm of the organization for decades. Beginning in the 1910s, then called the Young Women's Auxiliary, this group raised money to pay for the home's nurses, furniture, daily wares, and entertainment for the residents. The group ceased major fundraising campaigns in the 1960s, and by the 1980s the Auxiliary primarily functioned to plan events and provide companionship. In addition, the group encouraged community supporters and members to contribute to the Auxiliary's annual fund drive and presented a check to the West End Home for Ladies Healthcare Center each year from 1983 to 2007.[18]

The Auxiliary's budget had always remained separate from the Board of Directors as the two funds were used for different purposes. The group's account was wisely and quietly invested over the course of seventy-five years—guided by the leadership of the Auxiliary's treasurers and local banking firms. Ironical-

The painting of the West End Avenue home was moved to the new West End Home Foundation office on Kenner Avenue in 2011.

ly, their successful financial management made the consolidation of accounts (between the Board of Directors and Auxiliary) more complicated. Despite the longstanding clear demarcation of duties and obligations of each group, many in the Auxiliary desired a greater voice in the fate of the residential home and the long-term direction of the WEHF. With several million dollars in the Auxiliary's accounts, some in the volunteer group wanted to keep the Vanderbilt Place facility open, despite the impracticable costs and the lack of long-term viability. Others in the Auxiliary simply wanted to keep the accounts separate as the funds had been raised and invested independently.

A lack of communication had existed between the two groups for decades. At times, a lack of appreciation also caused hurt feelings when, for example, the Board passed down directives or when the Auxiliary made changes to the physical facility. In 2007, the Board voted to merge all budgets and financial assets between the Auxiliary and the Board to secure the future of the organization. Though well-intentioned, the decision was not without controversy. At an Auxiliary meeting held in April 2007, Gayle Elam Smith, who served on the Board and Auxiliary, resigned from the Board of Directors in opposition to the merger of the two accounts. Other Auxiliary members also left the meeting disappointed. Though both sides remained passionate and sincere in their desire to do what was best for the residents and the home, the transition "did not bring out the best in people," said Jean Dobson Farris, who was Vice-President of the Board at the time.[19]

Despite certain objections by some in the Auxiliary, the merger was necessary for several reasons. Most significantly, in order to continue as a grant foundation and to retain its status as a 501(c)(3), all accounts related to the West End Home Foundation were legally required to be submitted under one tax identification number. Second, the Board of Directors recognized, after extensive counsel with the WEHF's legal and accounting teams, that the time had come to move the remaining residents to a third-party facility. Finally, the

WEHF's influence as a positive force for good in the elder care community was best served if the organization united under the governance of the Board of Directors without an Auxiliary association.

After eight years of growing pains, including the shift from home to foundation and the formal dissolution of the Auxiliary in 2007, the West End Home Foundation Board of Directors moved forward with plans to move the remaining nine residents from Vanderbilt Place. One final difficult decision remained: determining the how, when, and where in choosing a new home and selling the Vanderbilt Place property. The foundation was obligated to provide a suitable living arrangement and healthcare, but more importantly, the Board loved the ladies and wanted them to remain happy and healthy. Resident Shelley Blitch had one condition for moving, noted Gayle Deerborn Vance. "Absolutely no men," said Blitch, who added, "They are a lot of trouble, believe me, I know."[20]

The Final Move

After careful consideration, the Board chose the Blakeford as the new home for the nine remaining residents, who stayed together as a community and moved into a newly constructed wing in April 2009. The Board also provided new furniture for the ladies' rooms and common areas in addition to the residents' own special belongings. The new Blakeford wing was built at a cost of $500,000 and paid for by the WEHF. The negotiations were largely handled by Barbara Cannon who was hired to help with the transition. A trained healthcare professional, Cannon spent months in consultation with local retirement communities and Nashville's healthcare leaders in search of the best fit for the remaining residents. Jean Farris noted, "Barbara helped to navigate a system that needed someone with expertise in the field. She was a nurse and a businesswoman. Enlisting her during the transition was a very good thing."[21] In addition to Farris and Cannon, other Board members crucial to this phase of the WEHF included Gayle Deerborn Vance, Gray Oliver Thornburg, Peggy Smith Warner, Drake Thompson Calton, Jane Chadwell Deloney, Fran Keltner Hardcastle, Carole Minton Nelson, and Mary Herbert Kelly.

The move itself was bittersweet for many involved. Administrative assistant Peggy Miller recalled, "I had an automobile accident just before the move and was unable to return to work until after the ladies had gone to the Blakeford. To be honest, it was a gift to miss the move; it would have been too hard. When I returned to Vanderbilt Place, my first day back at work, it felt so empty. I was so fond of the residents and the home. I made it to my desk, sat down, and cried."[22] Particularly heart-tugging was resident Eleanor Hersh's request to remain behind after the other ladies departed for the Blakeford. She asked to have lunch, and the staff obliged. Vance recalled, "Mrs. Hersh sat in the dining hall, eating Teresa's killer chicken salad" before closing the door for the last time.[23]

Amid great change for the "final nine," two WEHF staff members accepted offers of employment through the Blakeford—providing a sense of comfort and familiarity. Terronda Henderson and Gina Johnson, both nurses who had worked at the home for several years, were beloved by residents. When the ladies learned that Henderson and Johnson would be on staff at the Blakeford, "They could not have been happier."[24] Terronda Henderson recalled, "[The move] was really hard for most of the residents because the ladies did not know what to expect. I was glad I could stay with them to

Gina Johnson, Lilly Crane,
and Teresa Jones, 2010.

continue their care."[25] The home's last director, Randy Cornwell also maintained a relationship with the residents after their move. After completing certification as a healthcare consultant, the WEHF continued his employment on a subcontractor basis.

Trip to the Harley Davidson store and showroom: Ruth Beaver, Peggy Williams, Rita Lush, Lillian Harley, Louise Hobbs, Charlene Bomer, Bettye Moore, Muriel King, 2003.

Peggy Miller, who remained the foundation's administrative assistant until her retirement in 2016, also visited the ladies regularly and maintained her close relationship with these special women.[26] Miller was the go-to person when issues arose with the ladies at the Blakeford. Once she was asked to talk to Mrs. Hersh about her "strong language" with the Blakeford staff after Hersh's repeated complaints about not getting the *New York Times* first thing in the morning as she had at Vanderbilt Place. Board members described Miller as "a mediator and a patient-advocate who would go to bat for any one of them. They loved, loved, loved her."[27] The Board also depended heavily on Miller, who paid the bills, processed grant applications, and was the main point of communication between the community and the Board.

In addition to Miller, there was another Peggy who served as a patient-advocate after the move. Peggy Williams, who served as an LPN in the WEHF Healthcare Center and later the home's transportation director, visited the ladies twice weekly at the Blakeford. She did their shopping, made deliveries, and sometimes "just took them out for a drive to give them a change of scenery," according to Miller. A dedicated staff member and friend to all for thirty years,

Williams "stayed with them until the last lady passed away."[28] Board members agreed: "Peggy Williams was amazing, and her dedication to the ladies after the closure of the home reflected her unconditional love and support."[29]

There was also a concerted effort to take care of the staff when the home closed. The WEHF employed twenty-seven full-time employees in 2009 when the "final nine" moved to the Blakeford. The Board of Directors provided several options to the staff. They helped set up small businesses, paid for certification or coursework needed for employment searches, and offered retirement packages based on length of service. "We were as generous as we could be, and we wanted to be generous—because we had such a great staff," noted Gayle Deerborn Vance. Teresa Jones started a catering business after the home closed, but sadly lost her battle with cancer in 2011. Other staff members, such as Tami Scott, Frances Ducrest, and Jane Amonett transitioned to home healthcare and other positions. Sue Duncan, one of the home's longest serving nurses retired before the move. Duncan dutifully and lovingly worked as a registered nurse for the WEHF for nearly thirty years.

Sue Duncan served as a nurse for the Old Woman's Home and WEHF for nearly thirty years.

One of most difficult good-byes for the residents and Board members was Alfred Faria, who retired after serving for over twenty years as the head of maintenance and grounds. On Faria's relationship with the residents, Vance reminisced, "If one of the ladies was upset about something in her room, he took care of her. He was very protective and a great handyman at the home. He thought they were his ladies too."[30] The Board of Directors also depended on Faria to help with matters and issues that ranged from the small to the serious. One light-hearted moment involved Faria and Jean Dobson Farris in their attempt to catch a rat. Jean set a trap and caught it, but her success led to a potentially larger rodent problem. Alfred asked Jean, "What did you use to set the trap?" Jean answered, "Krispy-Kreme doughnuts,"

Alfred Faria and resident
Shelley Blitch, 2008.

to which Alfred replied, "I see I need to do this from now on."[31] Alfred Faria and many other former staff members continued to meet monthly from 2009 to 2011, until the sale of Vanderbilt Place, to check-in and catch up.

The Blakeford was chosen, in large part, because of its reputation as the "premier provider of senior living options in Nashville" based on an "extended family" model.[32] It also delivered a complete system of care, offering "the services you need when you need them," which ranged from independent living to skilled nursing care.[33] As part of the terms of the agreement, the Blakeford also pledged to maintain an all-female policy for the wing until after the passing of the last resident. This requirement was based on requests by the ladies who "had made a commitment to single-gender living and wanted it to stay that way."[34]

For the next four years, the remaining residents received ongoing care and support from a multidisciplinary team of professionals at the Blakeford. "By the time we moved to the Blakeford, none of the ladies were approved for independent living. They all went into assisted living and shortly thereafter nursing care," Jean Dobson Farris noted.[35] According to Terronda Henderson, "Everyone adjusted well and the WEHF made sure all the needs of the ladies were met. The biggest complaint was the food, but then again, no one could cook like Theresa." Henderson also noted that the "Board members were

Nettie Jane Langhans, Eleanor Hersh, and Jean Dobson Farris at the Blakeford, 2012.

very friendly and many came to the Blakeford for visits." With the loss of the Auxiliary, many Board members became more involved in the daily lives of the ladies. Moreover, life in the private facility did not diminish the WE-HF's commitment to steadfast support: "The ladies remained the Board's top priority until after the last resident passed away. We often cut back on giving grants because the remaining ladies needed more," stated Farris.[37]

Mrs. Eleanor Hersh was 102 years and six months when she died in May 2012, and the last resident, Lillian Harley, passed away April 2013, four years after the move to Blakeford. Mrs. Hersh and Miss Harley's deaths

One of the ladies' favorite entertainers, Bill Sleeter with Lillian Harley, 2008.

marked a sentimental and significant moment for the foundation. They were the last of more than five hundred women who found security, friendship and support through the home. While there was sadness for their loss and the end of 122-year history of residential care, there was also a sense of renewal as the WEHF looked to translate its original mission into an effective senior-care strategy designed to meet twenty-first century needs.

Returning to its Roots

In the early 2000s, the West End Home Foundation adopted a motto that articulated the organization's expanded mission: "The first to lend a helping hand, the last to turn away" was, in many ways, a declaration that returned the WEHF to its roots—as a charitable corporation whose sole purpose was to improve the lives of vulnerable members of the senior population.[38]

Gayle Deerborn Vance summarized the work of the Board, particularly after the 2009 closure of the home: "We went from being a Board that didn't act very quickly to one that did. We became involved in issues of senior advocacy. It was a road that perhaps we did not ex-pect, but we embraced it as part of our mission."[39] The success-ful transition and move was due, in large part, to the heroic efforts and fortitude of Jean Dobson Farris, who served as President of the Board from 2009 to 2011. Jean Ward Oldfield artic-ulated the importance of Farris's leadership: "I think Jean had a

Luncheon at Centennial Club with current and former Board and Auxiliary members, 2014. Fran Tarkington, Bettie Sue McNeilly, and N. Courtney Hollins.

Robert and Bettie Sue McNeilly at
WEHF archival exhibit reception, 2014.

far-reaching vision for the future of the
West End Home Foundation and meticulously researched each step needed
to move from a residential business to
an entity that used their assets to serve
seniors throughout the region. Her extensive research and tireless preparation
helped provide answers for the Board
members to weigh all of the pros and
cons in determining the foundation's direction."[40] New members to the Board after
2011 expanded the depth and breadth of experience needed to shape and sharpen
the WEHF's future direction. Some of these new members included Vanita Lytle-Sherrill, Dr. Arie L. Nettles, Cammie Turner Rash, Luanne Pitts Waltemath, N.
Courtney Hollins, Kim Sumner Hardin, and Anne Z. Morgan.

In September 2011, the buildings and property at 2818 Vanderbilt Place were
sold to Vanderbilt University for $5 million, and the WEHF moved to a new office
space on Kenner Avenue, two miles west. Even as the Board of Directors continued
its care of the remaining ladies at the Blakeford, they simultaneously turned their
attention to grantmaking. After the deaths of the last two ladies, the Board shifted
into high gear with its expanded organizational mission and structure. In fact, in
changing from residential to nonresidential services, the WEHF has perhaps never
been more true to its original mission. As Jean Dobson Farris noted, "Because we
were able to move from direct services to indirect services (through grants) we were
able to do so much for so many more."[41] The Board of Directors endorsed a similar
sentiment: "With the end of an era comes new opportunities. It also provides us
with the opportunity to renew the promise of our founding principles."[42]

The foundation first issued grants in 2002, giving 5 percent of the endowment
annually to organizations that improve the quality of life of seniors through advocacy, food, housing, health, and transportation services. Over $7.1 million in grant

funding was disbursed to agencies in the Middle Tennessee region by the WEHF from 2002 to 2014. Also in 2014, the WEHF hosted a luncheon at the Centennial Club of Nashville that represented an intersectional moment. Celebrating both the organization's tradition and progress, several members of the former Auxiliary and Board reminisced and recorded their memories. The event also unveiled the WEHF's new logo and website. Past President Gray Thornburg called it a "historical event...to celebrate the life of our ladies and to reintroduce ourselves as an important charitable non-profit corporation dedicated to the care of seniors."[43]

From 2014–2016, the WEHF distributed an additional $4.1 million in grants to direct service providers and programs designed to address issues related to elder care. In 2016 alone, grant awards totaling nearly $1.7 million were given to twenty-eight agencies serving Davidson and the six surrounding counties (Cheatham, Sumner, Williamson, Robertson, Rutherford, Wilson). In addition, the organizations and projects awarded grants have also increased from

Luncheon at Centennial Club with current and former
Board and Auxiliary members, 2014.

just over ten in 2011 to nearly thirty in 2016. Grant recipients in the 2016 class represented the WEHF's most ambitious agenda in addressing and advocating for seniors on a wide range of issues:

Alive Hospice: Capital funds for a hospice residence in Rutherford County

Arc of Davidson County: Assistance to individuals with short-term emergency housing issues

Alzheimer's Association: Consultation and education to those affected by Alzheimer's Disease

Bethlehem Centers: Meals on Wheels program for Nashville senior citizens

Council on Aging of Greater Nashville: Creation of a senior specific transportation program

Domestic Violence Program: Emergency services (shelter, counseling, transportation, legal assistance) for elderly victims of domestic violence in Rutherford County

Faith Family Medical: Healthcare for seniors including medical exams and counseling services

FiftyForward: Congregate meals, health and wellness programs and transportation for Bordeaux facility

Gilda's Club: Psycho-social support for seniors impacted by cancer

Interfaith Dental Clinic: Comprehensive and emergency dental care for seniors

Legal Aid Society: Educational seminars and legal services with a focus on long-term care options, advanced care directives, powers of attorney

Martha O'Bryan Center: Emergency Food Bank, Meals on Wheels, access to counseling

Matthew 25: Renovation of rooms at residential facility
for veterans

Mental Health America: Funding for the Centerstone Research
Institute for scale and evaluation of Just the Facts program

Mid-Cumberland Human Resource Agency: Food costs for
4,615 meals planned by a registered dietician and distributed in the five counties contiguous to Davidson

Nashville Food Project: Nutritious made-from-scratch meals
for seniors

Nashville Public Television: Aging Matters programs: "Alzheimer's and Dementia" and "Elder Abuse" including website,
DVD and screenings

NeedLink Nashville: Once yearly assistance with utility deposits,
past-due or disconnected utilities, rent, and/or housing deposit

Rooftop Foundation: Emergency rental/mortgage assistance to
prevent homelessness

Second Harvest Food Bank: Funding specifically for "Frozen
Tray Pack Meals" and "Senior Nutrition Boxes"

Siloam Family Health: Affordable healthcare to uninsured and
underinsured senior citizens

St. Luke's Community House: Mobile Meals program, Senior
Club, Senior Friends

Tennessee Justice Center: Legal advocacy for applicants of
CHOICES program; identification of systemic problems;
advocacy for elder care reform

Tennessee Respite Coalition: Respite care for caregivers of patients aged sixty years and older

United Cerebral Palsy: Services and medical equipment to keep
seniors in their own homes

> Vanderbilt University Medical Center: Funding for phase one of
> a project to enroll nursing homes in online program enabling
> nontraditional staff to provide daily feeding assistance
>
> Westminster Home Connection: Housing repairs and mobility
> modifications to address safety concerns

These twenty-seven organizations credit the WEHF as essential to their work in elder care. Marsha Edwards, president of the Martha O'Bryan Center spoke of the role that the WEHF plays in the community, "Together we are making substantial and immeasurable change on the ability of seniors to transcend the effects of poverty."[44] Another example of the WEHF's positive influence on the community is Nashville Public Television's "Aging Matters" program—an initiative that addresses senior issues such as isolation, exploitation, and abuse. This community-based program focused on Middle Tennessee includes documentaries, forums, and online resources and has received grants from WEHF. Beth Curley stated, "The West End Home Foundation has been a major supporter of Aging Matters for the last four years, and we're grateful for the generous support of this important project."[45]

Courtney Hollins, former Board president and current member, summed up the recent work of the WEHF, "In the last few years we have emerged as a foundation that is unparalleled in this community. Our 'business' and sole purpose is to support senior citizens in Davidson County and the contiguous counties."[46] According to public record, the West End Home Foundation's endowment also crossed a momentous threshold—surpassing the $40 million mark in 2017.

WEHF's Promising Future

From the Old Woman's Home to the West End Home for Ladies to the West End Home Foundation, more than two thousand women—including

Group picture before a performance at the West End Home for Ladies, 1989.

all residents, Board members, and Auxiliary members, have contributed to the organization's financial and institutional success. As WEHF Executive Director Dianne Oliver articulated: "These women not only had heart for what they were doing—they were smart. They put all the checks-and-balances in place, and they have done a phenomenal job of successfully managing a charitable foundation for over a century."[47] The WEHF's success also owes a great debt to the all-male Advisory Board as well as countless staff members who worked tirelessly to ensure the ladies' health and well-being.

Decades of hard work and long hours made possible the present-day organization now known as the West End Home Foundation. It was truly a labor of love. Reflecting now on 125 years, it is important to recognize the model of civic and compassionate service of all those connected to the organization. A historic foundation, forward-looking vision, committed Board, and strategic mission remain the primary indicators that ensure a promising future for the West End Home Foundation. Moreover, these factors will remain key as the senior care landscape continues to evolve.

Ruth Beaver was one of the more than five hundred women to enjoy her final years with the West End Home Foundation. Pictured here with Peggy Williams as she steps out of a limousine at the Grand Ole Opry, 2003.

In addition to the ever-evolving landscape of senior care, the nonprofit world has also changed dramatically over the last century. The Internal Revenue Service noted the historic foundations and growth of the tax-exempt sector: "Voluntary charitable and member-serving organizations have flourished in the United States since the country's genesis. In the early twentieth century, legislation that established the modern income tax system and concurrently granted tax-exempt status to certain organizations codified the relationship between the tax-exempt sector and government."[48] Currently, according to the National Center for Charitable Giving Statistics: "Nonprofit organizations [legally identified as 501(c)(3)] include everything from neighborhood associations that meet a couple of times a year and have no assets, to large universities and foundations with billions of dollars in assets."[49]

As private and public funding models have shifted over the last thirty years, the tax-exempt sector (or nonprofit industry) has grown significantly. In 1985,

Former and current employees and Board members enjoy a reception and the Nashville Public Library and an archival exhibit dedicated to the West End Home Foundation's history in 2014. Pictured are: Peggy Miller, former administrative manager, Mary Ann Smith, former dietary staff, Vanita Lytle-Sherrill, Board member, Sandra Thomas, former dietary staff, and Philomena Willis, former nursing staff.

there were 335,000 such organizations, and this number nearly tripled to 934,000 in 2004. By 2014, the United States registered more than 1.8 million active nonprofit agencies. The number of nonprofits in Tennessee is currently over 37,000, which places the state in the middle of the nonprofit pack with California (1) at nearly 230,000 and Wyoming (50) at 6,200 nonprofits.[50]

Charitable giving has risen in recent years and total assets held by nonprofit organizations topped $2 trillion in 2008.[51] To provide a snapshot of the increasing power of the nonprofit market—total contributions by individuals, foundations, bequests, and corporations reached $358 billion in 2014. However, contributions directed to nonprofits providing human services, including elder care, accounted for only 12 percent of giving despite an increase in and the projected growth of the senior population.[52] Such statistics reveal the essential role of the West End Home Foundation as a trusted intermediary between the community and the local organizations it supports.

The need for resources dedicated to supporting seniors will continue to increase in the coming decades. Based on demographic trends, as members of the Baby Boomer generation retire, the importance of the WEHF remains increasingly vital. Lester M. Salamon, professor at Johns Hopkins University and Director of the Center for Civil Society Studies stated: "Aging will be a key demographic trend for the foreseeable future. With average life expectancy rising in the United States…the size of the sixty-five-plus population will grow more than 75 percent, while the population paying payroll taxes will rise less than 5 percent between 2010 and 2030."[53]

These trends make the work of the WEHF ever more important. Former Board president and member Jean Dobson Farris noted, "The organization has come full circle and is now able to do more good, for more people, than we ever could have done within the old residential model. We have reinvented ourselves."[54] There is no question that WEHF is positioned to expand its role in Nashville and Middle Tennessee. With a growing number of older adults in the region, the West End Home Foundation is the only foundation in the region with an exclusive focus on senior issues.

The WEHF's focus on seniors was strengthened in January 2016 with the appointment of Dianne Oliver, the foundation's first executive director. She has a degree in gerontology and has worked in the nonprofit sector for more than thirty years in a variety of community planning, research, and grantmaking positions.[55] As incoming director, Oliver was wholly impressed: "I had the good fortune of coming

Executive Director Dianne Oliver and Administration and Technology Manager Cindy Dickinson.

into an organization that had been incredibly well-managed by a volunteer Board of Directors. The level of accountability and professionalism was surpassed only by the Board's passion and dedication to improving the lives of seniors."[56] Oliver adds a wealth of professional expertise in nonprofit management to the foundation's rich and proud leg-

Current Executive Committee of the Board of Directors. (L to R): N. Courtney Hollins, Kim Hardin, Margaret Smith, Peggy Craig, and Sallie Norton.

acy. Her experience also allows the WEHF to become more strategic and forward thinking in how it allocates money and achieves greater accountability in measuring outcomes of grant recipient funding for issues related to elder care.

One way that the organization has transitioned to a new model is the Board's decision to designate specific "Impact Areas." These identified categories are used to guide the WEHF as it seeks to further develop its infrastructure and the efficiency of grant making and other efforts that comprehensively improve the system of care for senior adults in Middle Tennessee. "Impact Areas" include a broad spectrum of programs related to advocacy, socialization, food/nutrition, healthcare, housing, transportation, wellness, and education. Organizations whose services fall within these areas are eligible for grants, but they must be 501(c)(3) and demonstrate the capacity to deliver services that achieve meaningful and measurable outcomes. The expanded grant application process, financial oversight, and annual reports created by Oliver and the Board of Directors have increased the transparency and effectiveness of the WEHF's generous funding to dozens of Middle Tennessee nonprofits.

Most recently the WEHF has been appointed to serve on a statewide consortium charged with distributing $35 million to projects that serve seniors throughout Tennessee. The funds resulted from settlement of Davidson County Chancery Court cases 11-1548-III and 12-1283-III (*State of Tennessee v. Senior-Trust and ElderTrust*) involving the liquidation of two nursing homes in Middle Tennessee. The appointment to the consortium came after three years of active involvement by WEHF in court proceedings, serving for part of that time as *amicus curiae* (friend of the court). WEHF advocated throughout the process that the funds be used exclusively to benefit seniors.

The foundation's involvement started in December of 2013 when Luanne Pitts Waltemath, Board member and Gray Oliver Thornburg, then President of the Board, learned of these funds. With the blessing of the Board of Directors, C. K. McLemore (WEHF attorney) and Jay Grannis (WEHF accountant), Thornburg prepared and hand delivered a grant request to the Attorney General's office.[57] The Attorney General's proposed plan for distribution of the funds did not include WEHF but that plan was later overturned by the Davidson County Chancery Court. Due in part to WEHF's advocacy efforts, Chancellor Ellen Hobbs Lyle, after thorough review and study, proclaimed that the funds be designated for senior serving programs and be administered by a statewide consortium including private funders and the Tennessee Commission on Aging and Disability (TCAD). WEHF is one of the five granting organizations in the consortium along with the Memorial Foundation, HCA Foundation, Assisi Foundation of Memphis, and United Way of Greater Knoxville.

This public private partnership is an opportunity for WEHF to expand its reach by participating in a statewide process that will significantly impact the elder care system. Dianne Oliver concluded, "To receive $35 million for the benefit of seniors is a once in a lifetime gift. This totally aligns with our mission, and we are committed to providing whatever resources are necessary to help the process succeed."[58] The WEHF's primary focus remains individual grants to direct service providers in Middle Tennessee, but participation in the consortium has allowed the WEHF to emerge as a statewide leader in elder care.

Reception to celebrate 125th Anniversary. From left to right: N. Courtney Hollins, Sallie Norton, Phyllis Heard, Paula Hughey.

The West End Home Foundation is today a catalyst for meaningful and lasting change for the betterment of the region's senior adults. The foundation is a voice that advocates for an aging population and facilitates a more comprehensive system of care. Today, decisions are conducted by a committed Board of Directors comprised of community and professional leaders that bring a wealth of diverse experience. Longtime Board and Auxiliary member, Jean Ward Oldfield articulated the promise of the organization's future:

> The WEHF is a big business and its leadership has been thoughtfully put together....My greatest hope is that the WEHF receives the recognition they deserve as the premier organization in Middle Tennessee for taking care of seniors. Beyond giving grants, I also hope the WEHF is recognized for their ideas and

connections in improving the overall network of services designed to help senior citizens.[59]

Careful oversight, active investment, and a diversified portfolio provides the basis for the WEHF's promising future—as it did in the past. Moreover, the WEHF's leadership and staff maintain a growth mind-set that combines good thinking, intentional action, and effective implementation. The organization may no longer deliver direct services or residential care, but it serves as an engaged community partner. The WEHF not only provides grants but sponsors community forums, promotes educational programming, and raises public awareness to improve the lives of all Middle Tennessee seniors. "We are a convener and collaborator of expertise when it comes to the needs of seniors," said N. Courtney Hollins.[60] Gray Thornburg added, "And we have the knowledge to fund and support those needs."[61]

Reception to celebrate 125th Anniversary. From left to right: Margaret Smith, Susan Kaestner, Bill Farris, Kim Hardin, Mary Ellen Pethel, Arie Nettles, Gray Thornburg.

T. S. Eliot wrote in 1940:

> Home is where one starts from. As we grow older
> The world becomes stranger, the pattern more complicated…
> There is a time for the evening under starlight,
> A time for the evening under lamplight…
> Love is most nearly itself
> When here and now cease to matter.[62]

The West End Home Foundation has changed names and locations, said hello and good-bye to many beloved members of its extended family and community, and adapted when needed and when faced with a changing society. But two things, as Eliot reminds us, have endured throughout this noble organization's history and remain central to its identity and guiding principles. The first is home—and the notion that there is no substitute for its comforts and the sense of security and belonging it brings. The second is love—particularly the unconditional and

The current front door of the WEHF office on Kenner Avenue.

unwavering support of seniors when they need it most, when "the world becomes stranger, the pattern more complicated." Because it is in that moment that "love is most nearly itself."

Special Ladies, Special Lives
Selected Former Residents

Whether the name was the Old Woman's Home, West End Home for Ladies, or West End Home Foundation, it was a place where all of the residents were special ladies who led special lives. Over five hundred residents benefited from the organization's commitment to senior women, which provided residential and end-of-life care for over 120 years. Biographical sketches representing a cross-section of women who lived at the home from the early 1900s to the early 2000s reflect the many different women for whom the organization existed to serve.

The work and record collection of Cindy Dickinson over a period of four years served as the basis for researching and writing about the lives of the women that follow. Dickinson's attention to detail, along with the information she compiled about the ladies of the home remains a historical treasure.

The Tavel Sisters: Pauline Marie, Isobel, Hellen

The Tavel family's journey to Nashville began in Switzerland. Paul Frederick Tavel was a bookbinder and horticulturalist who first came to Tennessee in 1844. Over the next eight years Paul traveled back and forth to Switzerland before deciding to move his family permanently to Nashville. His wife, Mary Helena Sabatini Tavel, and four children immigrated to the United States in 1852. At the time, Pauline Marie was eleven, Albert Berry was nine, Isobel was six, and Hellen was three. Mary Helena made the arduous journey from Switzerland to the United States with her four children while also pregnant. The couple welcomed a fifth child, Anne Eugenne, in 1852 just months

ALBERT B. TAVEL,
PUBLISHER AND DEALER IN
LAW BOOKS AND LEGAL STATIONERY
OF EVERY DESCRIPTION.
309 MARKET ST.   NASHVILLE, TENN.

Albert Tavel advertisement, c. 1910.

after the family's arrival in Nashville.[1] It is known that Paul's family was Swiss and Mary Helena's family was Italian, but how they met is not documented. The Tavels sought a new life filled with opportunity in the United States. Paul trained his only son, Albert, as an apprentice in bookbinding and printing.

Bookbinding and printing skills would be advantageous for Albert as Nashville's reputation as a southern publishing center grew considerably after the Civil War. Albert established a printing press business in 1873 with two partners. His firm, Tavel, Eastman, & Howell, also added cartography to its repertoire—publishing several famous early maps of Nashville including an 1879 Nashville Board of Health map covering downtown streets, districts, railroads, and landmarks. For the next thirty years Tavel & Howell, as they were later known, served as the official "Printers to the State of Tennessee" and published department reports, maps, directories, legislative acts, legal codes, court decisions, and so on.[2]

Albert purchased a home on Laurel Street, for his four sisters, just west of Union Station, and he lived nearby with his wife and children on Division Street. The sisters lived a charmed life in Nashville and were active in West End Methodist Church; however, they

Tavel Sisters, c. 1925.

remained single and did not have children. Anne Eugenne, died in 1918 at the age of fifty-five as a result of kidney failure, identified at the time as uremia.[3]

Aside from his business interests, Albert Tavel officially entered local politics when he was elected to the position of magistrate in 1888. Magistrates during this period acted as civil officers or lay judges who administered legal judgements for minor offenses.[4] Albert sought to make arrangements for the future for his remaining sisters after the death of Anne Eugenne, who was the youngest of the siblings. As an active member of the Masons, it was through these connections that Tavel and fellow members of the downtown Masonic Lodge raised enough money to endow two rooms in the Old Woman's Home for Tavel's three remaining sisters for $5,000.

Hellen, Pauline Marie, and Isobel were admitted to the Old Woman's Home in 1923, five years after their youngest sister's death. The Old Woman's Home on West End Avenue provided them with the comforts of home and prevented their separation in their final years. The Tavel sisters were the only three sisters to ever live in the home. Hellen died in 1928, Pauline Mary lived until 1931, and Isobel passed away in 1937 at the age of ninety. Their journey ended as it had begun—together.

Cora Haley Green Fitzhugh

Thomas Hardy, British author and intellectual (1840–1928) wrote in *Tess of the d'Urbervilles: A Pure Woman Faithfully Presented*: "The perfect woman, you see, was a working woman; not an idler; not a fine lady; but one who used her hands and her head and her heart for the good of others."[5] Cora Fitzhugh's life, work, and sense of purpose certainly embodied this sentiment.

Born in 1858 on the cusp of the Civil War, Cora Elizabeth Haley grew up in College Grove, Tennessee. She married Dr. Madison Green in the late 1870s, and the couple lived happily in College Grove until his death in 1883. Cora re-married in 1885, but her second husband, Abraham Fitzhugh, passed away six short years later. After the death of Abraham, she made a bold move some thirty-five miles away to Nashville in 1891 with her only child, Clifton H. Green. In 1903, Mrs. Fitzhugh joined McKendree Methodist Church, located in the heart of downtown Nashville. She remained a faithful member at McKendree for the rest of her life.

After working in various jobs downtown, Cora took another leap of faith and invested the sum of her savings to open her own restaurant in 1910.[6] "The Little Gem," as it was named, opened in the upstairs space of 327½ Union Street in downtown Nashville and catered to business-men looking for a midday meal. Her restaurant occupied prime real estate at the corner of Union Street and 4th Avenue between the Arcade shopping mall and Printer's Alley (an area with many venues, bars, and restaurants). For 15 cents, patrons could have "soup, a good-sized roast beef slice, mashed potatoes, slaw, pickle, and choice of coffee, iced tea, or milk."[7] One former

Cora Elizabeth Fitzhugh, 1949.

patron said, "She gave her restaurant a real home-like atmosphere." Local historian Stanley F. Horn recalled, "For those who could afford it, Mrs. Fitzhugh's dining room…served a bounteous, family-style meal, 'all you can eat,' for a quarter."[8]

Her restaurant drew many regular customers, and her status as an entrepreneur and restaurateur was well known throughout Nashville for more than fifteen years. Mrs. Fitzhugh was precisely the type of woman for whom the Old Woman's Home existed—industrious, pious, hardworking, and well connected. As Mrs. Fitzhugh approached her final years and needed more assistance than her family could provide, many of her former patrons and fellow church members recommended that she be accepted to the Old Woman's Home.

Cora Fitzhugh lived independently until the age of eighty-nine when she joined the OWH extended family in 1948. She was welcomed with open arms, and just six month after she moved into the West End Avenue facility, the Auxiliary threw her a special birthday party to celebrate her ninetieth birthday. Cora Fitzhugh's friends and OWH residents recalled that she had a motherly, fun-loving personality that drew others to her.[9] Cora Fitzhugh's life was certainly full of purpose. Her life also reflects the power of opportunity when combined with a love for God and serving others. She had a light, and she let it shine.

Mollie Wright Shook and Lucy A. Foreman

No one would have guessed that Mollie Wright Shook and Lucy Foreman would end up living out their lives together at the Old Woman's Home on West End Avenue, but it came as a great comfort to those who knew them. Mollie and Lucy had been fellow parishioners at McKendree Methodist Church and friends for more than thirty years. Mollie began her career at the Methodist Publishing House South in downtown Nashville in 1903 and worked there until 1936. From 1926 to 1956, Lucy also held a position as a full-time staff member in publishing for the denomination's Sunday School Division from 1903 until 1956.

Mollie was born in Memphis in 1870; Lucy was born in Nashville in 1877. While they did not grow up in the same city, they shared similar childhoods as the South experienced dramatic change during the era of Reconstruction (1865–1877) following the Civil War. Mollie and Lucy attended public school in Memphis and Nashville respectively. Mollie married Alfred George Shook in 1887, but just one year after moving to Nashville in 1904, he tragically passed away. The two

women often attended McKendree together, found many things in common,
and thus formed a solid friendship,
one widowed and one unmarried. Both
Mrs. Shook and Miss Foreman worked
diligently to further causes that educated and improved the lives of others.

In addition to working at the
Methodist Publishing House, Mollie
Shook served as chairman of the Red
Cross Sewing Unit for twenty years
and led sewing efforts for soldiers
during World War II. Also active as a
member of Scarritt College Aid Soci-

Mollie Wright Shook, 1955.

ety, Mrs. Shook helped to raise money for Christian missions for more than fifty years. In addition, Mrs. Shook was active in the Davidson County Anti-Tu-
berculosis Association. In 1949, she wrote and published the following call for
donations for the Red Cross and Scarritt College just before Easter Sunday:

> While cleaning your house are you selling and giving away your
> unused clothes, books, magazines and pieces of furniture? Help
> us help others…Because there WAS a resurrection, the heart of
> the world which once rejected the Savior turns to that event as
> the focal point of all mortal and immortal hope. Jesus prom-
> ised, "Because I live ye shall live also." So while CLEANING
> HOUSE, remember this message.[10]

Lucy Foreman did not work in the same Methodist publishing office as
Mollie Shook, but she remained active as a published author and gifted teacher.

Lucy A. Foreman, 1958.

She taught Christian education classes across Tennessee and the United States. Miss Foreman believed that "often a lesson could be taught more effectively through the use of a story. She was proficient in the art of storytelling and wrote a number of short books."[11] Published works included *Men and Women at Work in the Small Church* (1943), *The Superintendent of the One Room Church School* (1943), *Adults at Work in the Small Church* (1941), and *The Church Board of Education in the Small Church* (1936).[12]

At the age of seventy-two, Mollie Shook applied for admission to the Old Woman's Home. With glowing recommendations from her church and community, she was accepted and moved to the West End Avenue home in 1942. Twelve years later, Lucy Foreman found herself in similar circumstances at the age of seventy-nine. With one brother who lived outside of Nashville, Lucy was recommended to the OWH Board of Directors by McKendree Methodist Church members and other friends. Without hesitation, the OWH admitted her, and Lucy joined Mollie at the Old Woman's Home in May 1956. The two friends spent eight years at the OWH before Mollie Shook passed away in 1964. Lucy's death came just two years later in 1966. They were special ladies who led special lives both as individuals and as fellow residents.

Susan Elsie Morrison Riley

In a letter to Board of Directors President Bettye Sue Parrish McNeilly, Elizabeth A. Shapiro paid resident Susan Riley the highest possible compliment:

"She was…the most unselfish person we have ever known."[13] The Shapiro family certainly knew Mrs. Riley well enough to attest to the strength of her character and generosity. The family first met Susan Riley in the 1950s when Dr. John Shapiro, who served as a Vanderbilt professor of medicine and pathologist volunteered at the Nashville Rescue Mission. It was there that he first witnessed the kind and selfless service of Mrs. Riley. She formed a friendship so strong with the family that they asked her to move in with them after she could no longer work, and Mrs. Riley lived and traveled with the Shapiros from 1954 through the mid-1960s.[14]

Born in Missouri in 1895, Susan Morrison Riley's family moved to Oklahoma when she was a young girl. There she grew up at a time when Oklahoma was simply called "Indian Territory," and her father, William Allen Morrison was the only person in town who could read and write. Consequently, he was responsible for all the correspondence with Washington D.C. regarding business matters related to federal legislation related to territory. Specifically, William Morrison helped his

Susan Elsie Morrison Riley, c. 1975.

local community understand what was known as the Oklahoma Land Rush of 1889.[15] Susan's mother died when she was a small child, and her stepmother was a Cherokee Indian. Such marriages were not uncommon in the area since Oklahoma was the largest Cherokee reservation in the nation (and the destination of the infamous Trail of Tears in the 1830s). Her stepmother "taught Susan and her brothers that illness was a sign of weakness, and one must never remain in bed."[16] Susan took this lesson to heart, rarely missing any event whether it be work, church, bingo, a party, or simply Sunday dinner.

Mrs. Riley had no formal schooling until she was twelve. For the next nine years she alternated attending school as a student and as a teacher. She ultimately graduated from Oklahoma Baptist University, where she met her husband John Charles Riley who was a seminary student at the university. After their marriage in 1917, Reverend Riley was called as a pastor to a Baptist church in Lebanon, Tennessee.[17]

Susan and John had one daughter, Carol Riley Powers, before John passed away suddenly in 1936. Widowed in her forties, she found a way to support herself while still faithfully serving those less fortunate. Mrs. Riley worked for approximately twenty years as a teacher and matron at the Tennessee Baptist Orphanage, later called the Baptist Children's Home in Williamson County, Tennessee. Ironically, the orphanage also began in 1891, the same year the Old Woman's Home opened its doors on Cedar Street in Davidson County. Riley was remembered as a woman who spent most of her meager salary on "extras" for the children or the orphanage.[18]

Susan was admitted to the Old Woman's Home on June 25, 1969, at the age of seventy-four and would spend the last twelve years of her life at the West End Avenue facility. Elizabeth Shapiro concluded: "I believe you have never had a resident more in love with 2811 West End Avenue than Susan Riley. I think Mrs. Riley was so happy...and so grateful to be there."[19] Susan Riley was one of the last women to live out her life at the West End facility before the move to Vanderbilt Place.

Ellen Jane Douglas Jones Ginn

In a letter to the Board of Directors just before her death in 1982, Ellen Jane Douglas Jones Ginn wrote: "I want to state again that I thank God and you dear people at the Old Woman's Home for giving me this wonderful place among such lovely and gracious people to spend so many years of my remaining life with. May God reward each and every one for their kindness and patience, is my prayer."[20] Ellen Ginn's words reflected the sentiment of most residents who called the Old Woman's Home—home. However, Mrs. Ginn's life personifies the type of woman for whom the Old Woman's Home was established.

Born in 1878 in Nashville to John Griffith Jones, who immigrated to the United States from Wales, England, and Fannie Eugenie Bowers of Nashville— Ellen had reason to be proud of her family's accomplishments. Her father was a mason who was subcontracted to oversee the stonework during the construction of the Tennessee State Capitol. Famed architect William Strickland recruited Jones for his superb craftsmanship in the mid-1840s, and Jones moved to Nashville where he met and married Fannie Bowers. The cornerstone of the capitol was laid on July 4, 1845, and the building was completed fourteen years later in 1859. Jones remained in Nashville as a builder, and thirty years later he was hired to help build another Nashville landmark—the Ryman Auditorium. Ellen's mother, Fannie, was active in the Baptist church and instilled in her daughter a love of service and faithful devotion. She attended Third Baptist Church as a child with her mother and would remain a lifelong member of the Baptist church.

Ellen was well educated for a young woman in the late nineteenth century. She attended secondary school at the Fogg School (today Hume-Fogg High School), Boscobel College (a local women's school), and the Nashville Conservatory of Music. She was an accomplished vocalist. Her passion for

Ellen Jane Douglas Ginn, c.1980.

education, music, and religious mission work would lead to a career with the Tennessee Baptist Convention.

Ellen Jane Douglas Jones married Max "Maxie" Medison Ginn in 1903. Maxie Ginn passed away in 1928 after twenty-five years of marriage. Seven years before her husband's death, Ellen took a job as an office secretary at the Tennessee Baptist Convention as part of the Auxiliary Women's Missionary Union (WMU)—a position she would hold until 1957. In addition to her office duties she was also paid to write, teach, and lecture on behalf of the WMU, whose purpose remains the education and involvement of children, youth, and adults in the "cause and support of Christian missions at home and abroad."[21] In addition to her work with the Tennessee Baptist Convention, she served as a Sunday school teacher for most of her adult life.

Mrs. Ginn clearly liked to keep things simple. After the passing of her husband, she moved to an apartment across the street from the Tennessee Baptist office. In an interview, she said, "I had the same desk and the same chair for thirty-six years and I lived across the street from the office until they decided to tear down the building,"[22] The year after she retired, Ellen decided to document the history of the state's WMU and wrote *As I Saw It: Seventy-Year History of the Tennessee Women's Missionary Union* in 1958 under the pen name Douglas Jones Ginn.[23] The book continues to serve as a vital record and account of the early history of the WMU in Tennessee. (Today's national WMU is the largest Protestant missions organization for women in the world.)[24]

In 1968 the Tennessee Baptist Convention moved to the suburb of Brentwood in neighboring Williamson County. Less than two years later, Mrs. Ginn was given notice that her apartment building was slated for demolition. With the encouragement of friends and members of the Judson Memorial Baptist Church congregation, Mrs. Ginn applied and was accepted into the Old Woman's Home just before turning ninety. No one would have imagined that she would live thirteen more years at the home. Interviewed on her 101st birthday on local news outlets, Ellen Ginn attributed her longevity to having led a healthy Christian life. She joked that her interest in historic buildings and structures her father helped construct was because "I don't want to be the only old thing left in town."[25] Ginn passed away in 1982 at the age of 103—a rich and full life indeed.

Mary Elizabeth Cayce

Those who knew Mary Elizabeth Cayce knew her as a force of nature and woman of purpose. She also holds the distinction of being the only woman to serve as the president of the Auxiliary and a member of the Board of Directors before ultimately living as a resident at the home.

Born in 1909, Cayce was the daughter of James Ambrose Cayce Jr. and Mary East Cayce. Her father was a prominent business-man and founder of the Nashville Chamber of Commerce. Both Mary Elizabeth Cayce and her father were lifelong activists who ad-vanced causes dedicated to improving afford-able housing and education.

With the passage of the first United States Housing Act in 1937, the citizens of Nashville began work to establish a municipal housing au-thority. Following a vote of approval by the Nashville City Council on October 31, 1938, the Nashville Housing Authority was formed, with its first meeting held November 9, 1938. James Cayce was its first Board Chairman. In May 1939, an application was submitted to the U.S. Housing Authority for the con-

Mary Elizabeth Cayce, 1984.

struction of two subsidized housing developments named Boscobel Heights and the J. C. Napier Homes. Boscobel Heights was later renamed in honor of Mary Elizabeth's father, who died during construction. The housing development still bears his name: James A. Cayce Homes.[26]

Mary Elizabeth attended Miss Annie Allison's Preparatory School followed by the prestigious Ward-Belmont School. While a student at Ward-Belmont, Miss Cayce visited the Old Woman's Home often as groups from the school performed for the ladies there. Miss Cayce graduated from Ward-Belmont in 1928 and completed her bachelor's degree at George Peabody College for Teachers. She joined the Ward-Belmont faculty as a physical education teacher—a position she held from 1930 to 1945. She was also active in the movement to establish the Harpeth Hall School after the sudden closing of Ward-Belmont, and she served on the original Board of Trustees. On the campus of Harpeth Hall, the Mary Elizabeth Cayce Conference Room was named to honor her memory and contributions to the school, a place that she referred to as "my real interest and love."[27]

After her career as an educator, Miss Cayce followed in her father's footsteps in business to become a successful businesswoman. In 1945 she was named the Vice-President of B. H. Stief Jewelry Company, ultimately becoming the company's President and owner until her retirement from the company in 1970. However, in a 1974 feature *Tennessean* article entitled "Cayce Retired? Not on Your Life!" journalist Susan Brandau wrote: "Mary Elizabeth Cayce has retired in name only. For many years Vice-President of the old B. H. Stief Jewelry Company—'Cayce'—as she is known far and wide led the business to great success."[28] When asked about life after a career as a business executive, Cayce laughed and said,

> Retirement is marvelous but I'm busier now than when I worked. Scarcely a day passes without somebody calling to ask me what

to do about knives that need new blades or what to give for a 50th wedding anniversary. I just became president of the Polk Memorial Association. I knew less about Polk than anybody when I became president. But I've found out a lot about him including the fact that he's the only president we ever had who said at the beginning of his term of office that he wouldn't run again and didn't! So he didn't have to cater to special interests and wasn't obligated to anybody.[29]

Mary Elizabeth Cayce's position as a Nashville leader and philanthropist was a lifelong endeavor. She was connected, well-educated, versatile, proactive, and engaged. Miss Cayce used her status to advance causes that helped Nashvillians from all walks of life. Her community activism included several Boards of Trust and committees (in addition to the Old Woman's Home): United Giver's Fund, Red Cross, Duncanwood Day Care Center, Family and Childrens' Service, James K. Polk Memorial Association, Ladies Hermitage Association, Centennial Club, Belle Meade Country Club, Protestant Orphanage Foundation, YWCA, Harpeth Hall School, and Enworth School. Miss Cayce was an active member of Westminister Presbyterian Church. Most significantly, she was elected the first President of the Nashville Junior League in 1944.

Her involvement with the OWH began in 1970 following an invitation to join the Auxiliary after her retirement at the age of sixty-six. By 1974 she was the Auxiliary President and charged with fundraising. Miss Cayce later joined the OWH Board of Directors in the late 1970s. With her experience in business, her exper-

Phyllis Heard, Jane Deloney, Mary Elizabeth Cayce, c. 1988.

tise and advice was much needed as the organization approached a crossroads in regard to its facility, costs, and model of care. Following an accident, Miss Cayce decided to join the other women at the home she had helped for more than fourteen years. She moved into the West End Home for Ladies in 1984 with her longtime friend and employee Lillian Harley, where she remained until her death in 1998. Harley would live until 2013; she was the last lady to receive residential and medical care from the WEHF as part of the organization's traditional model of direct services.

Mary Elizabeth Cayce remained active in several organizations even after her move to the home. Notably she was awarded the Award of Merit from the American National Red Cross after thirty years of work with the organization. As she articulately summed it up: "Nashville is my home. My parents were volunteers. I have a feeling of obligation and pride in this community. There are so many worthwhile projects to work on. I am fundamentally interested in people. [Working in Nashville], I got to know people, young and old."[30] The West End Home Foundation acknowledges Mary Elizabeth Cayce as a devoted civic leader—nonprofit institutions across the city would agree.

Mary McCullough Keith

Sixteenth-century English poet and scholar Philip Sydney poignantly wrote, "The ingredients of health and long life are great temperance, open air, easy labor, and little care [or worry]."[31] Mary McCullough Keith took Sydney's message to heart—living a rich, purposeful, and long life while making the most of its simple pleasures.

Miss Keith, affectionately known as "Culla," attended the Stokes School and Peabody College in the 1920s and 1930s. She excelled in the fine arts, and in addition to her gift as an artist, she was an avid reader and loved an-

imals. In her youth, Miss Keith enjoyed horseback riding and attending the opera with her grandmother.
Culla and her grandmother were
very close, visiting cities across the
country to hear their favorite vocal-
ists and performances. Miss Keith's
passion for opera was a lifelong affair; even after she could no longer

Mary McCullough Keith, c. 2000.

attend the opera, she often played her favorite records from her collection.[32]

Mary McCullough Keith's family ties to the West End Home Foundation
dated back to the organization's founding. She was the great-granddaughter
of Elizabeth Keith, the granddaughter of Walter and Emmy Ewing Keith, and
great-niece of Percy and Mary Belle Keith Maddin. Her parents, Walter and
Josephine Boensch Keith, as well as her siblings Walter Keith III, Emmy Keith
Frost, and Frances Keith Berson also supported the organization over the years.

When Josephine became ill, it was Mary McCullough who cared for her
mother, stating, "It was the busiest time of my life."[33] After the death of her
mother—there was no doubt that the West End Home for Ladies (later West
End Home Foundation) was the perfect new home for Culla. In fact, when
asked where she would move, she announced, "I know where I'm going, I'm going to the West End Home."[34] Mary McCullough Keith was admitted in 1990
at the age of sixty-nine.

Auxiliary member Janie Macey recalled, "Not only was her family very close
to the home, Culla was wonderful, easy to care for, and glad to have us to take
care of her."[35] She enjoyed reading books by prolific novelist Taylor Caldwell
(1900–1985), attending the tea parties hosted by the Auxiliary, and participating in Betty Nance's Bible study. Miss Keith passed away on February 24, 2007,
at the age of eighty-six, after living for seventeen years under the care and super-

Walter Keith Jr. pours tea for his daughter Mary McCullough Keith (right) and resident Rose Lee (left), 1991.

vision of the West End Home Foundation. Mary McCullough Keith will long be remembered for her "kindness, humor, and warm humanity."[36]

Her great-grandmother, Elizabeth Keith, would have been proud of the love and support Miss Keith received through the care of the West End Home Foundation. It seems only fitting that a member of the Keith family be one of the last residents to live in the organization's independent facility before the transition to the Blakeford and indirect services in 2009.

Eleanor May Herts Hersh

Esther, the revered ancient biblical figure, demonstrated that it is possible to achieve great success in life without giving up one's identity as a strong Jewish woman. Eleanor Hersh's life serves as a testament to Esther's legacy. Mrs. Hersh, while a woman of the world and accomplished in her own right, always maintained a servant's heart.

Mrs. Hersh was a "little bitty lady with a sparkle in her eye," according to longtime Board and Auxiliary member Jean Ward Oldfield.[37] That sparkle in her eye was evident from a young age. Born in 1909, the ever-precocious Eleanor embraced adventure as her family moved up and down the West Coast, first in Portland then Seattle and later to Los Angeles and Oakland. At the age of ten, the Herts family traveled extensively in the South Pacific and Asia; the eighteen-month trip was part of a business assignment for her father, Arthur Herman Herts, who worked for O. Armleder Motor Truck Company.[38] Their travel included time spent visiting Sydney, Melbourne, Shanghai, Tokyo, Java, and Hong Kong.[39] Eleanor and her sister even attended school in Sydney and Melbourne.

Following this and other trips that included Europe and India, the family moved to New York, where she attended Tarrytown Grammar School from 1920 to 1922. In 1923, the Herts moved to London where they would stay until 1939. Eleanor completed her education in European boarding schools. It is likely that the family moved back to the United States after Germany's invasion of Poland and the start of World War II.

As a young woman living in London in the 1930s, Eleanor Herts first became an entrepreneur when she opened a shop that manufactured and sold custom knitted sweaters and other garments. Another young woman, May MacDonald, was Eleanor's business partner. The shop's reputation spread throughout the city and attracted a high-end clientele. Prior to 1936, two of her most notable customers included King Edward VIII (formerly Duke of Windsor) with American socialite Wallis Simpson.

Eleanor Hersh on her 100th birthday, 2009.

After moving back to New York, Eleanor married Louis Hersh in 1943, and the newlyweds moved to Nashville where their daughter, Ann Hersh (Gilbert), was born. Three years later, they moved to New York City where Mrs. Hersh designed knitting and needlepoint patterns and sold sweaters to Lord and Taylor before becoming one of the first female traveling sales representatives selling craft kits to hobby shops in the states surrounding Pennsylvania.[40] After the death of her husband, Eleanor once again turned to her talents for business and knitting to support her daughter and mother. She worked full-time in a retail shop in addition to her sales career until the early 1970s. It was in the early 1970s that Mrs. Hersh moved back to Nashville, at the age of sixty-three. She opened a yarn shop in Green Hills and continued working at other local shops such as Angel Hair Yarns until the age of seventy-six.

Mrs. Hersh was admitted to the West End Home for Ladies on October 30, 1985, and instantly became one of the home's most endearing and resourceful residents. Any and every person who encountered Mrs. Hersh instantly recognized her unique individuality and insatiable spirit. While she no longer worked for pay, Eleanor Hersh continued to volunteer, as she had all of her life—teaching knitting and needlework to people of all ages. In addition to teaching classes at various yarn shops, she also taught at Hillsboro High School as part of an adult education program as well as senior citizens groups and children in local schools. She also volunteered for more than thirty years at the Gordon Jewish Community Center, National Council of Jewish Women, St. Thomas Hospital, and Cheekwood Botanical Garden. At the age of ninety-seven, Mrs. Hersh stated, "If I could drive, I'd do a lot more volunteer work. People don't volunteer enough here. You can always find something to do."[41] When there was no one to take her where she wanted to go, Mrs. Hersh rode the city bus. She also swam at the Jewish Community Center well into her nineties.

Eleanor Hersh, 2012.

While living at the West End Home for Ladies and later at the Blakeford, Mrs. Hersh was always on the go. The *WEHFL Newsletter* described Hersh in 1999, "A regular whirlwind, Eleanor is one person that everyone looks up to and respects for her enthusiasm, energy, and positive attitude about growing older."[42] Nettie

Jane Langhans, former president of the Auxiliary stated, "As she became more stooped, I had to bend over to interact with her at lunch or during a visit. But that didn't stop Mrs. Hersh from doing things and enjoying life."[43]

Her daughter, Ann Hersh Gilbert, captured what made Mrs. Hersh extraordinary: "My mother was full of curiosity and playfulness. She was creative and wise. She was stubborn and feisty…She was traditional and at the same time modern."[44] Eleanor's resolve was apparent in her final years of residence at the Vanderbilt Place facility. As the number of ladies dwindled, she refused to move from the third floor, and lived for more than two years as the top floor's sole resident. Former administrative assistant Peggy Miller stated, "Everyone begged her to move to be closer to other residents and staff. She adamantly refused."[45] In the last months of her life, Mrs. Hersh was admitted to Vanderbilt University Medical Center to be treated for pneumonia. Before being discharged Gayle Vance stated, "She called in the nurses and had a meeting. She thanked them for all they had done for her, and then she told them how the unit could be improved. That was Mrs. Hersh."[46] Six months shy of her 102nd birthday, Eleanor May Herts Hersh peacefully passed away at the Blakeford. All connected to the WEHF mourned her death but celebrated her life.

Timeline

Date	Description
1881	Nashville Relief Society formed by Fannie Battle and other prominent local citizens and churches.
1886	The first call for a home for children and elderly women with little or no family support.
1886	Death of Memucan Hunt Howard who designated the lead gift for the Old Woman's Home in his Last Will and Testament.
1887	Decision made to open a residential space for elderly women of "gentle birth," orphans, and "sewing girls" (female child laborers).
1889	Eliza Crostwaite, Fannie Battle, Sarah Childress Polk, Samuel and Elizabeth Keith, James and Martha Whitworth, Mr. and Mrs. L.H. Lanier, Judge John Lea, J.S. and Cynthia Reeves, William and Elizabeth Morrow, O.F. Noel, F.W. Waller, Arthus and Agnes Estill Colyar, and other leading families contribute funds to establish living facility for the "worthy poor" within Nashville Relief Society headquarters.
1889	Purchase of the Weller House on 136 Cherry Street for $12,000.
1889	Ten women are moved into the Weller House.

1891   "Home for Aged Women and Orphan Waifs" legally separates from the Nashville Relief Society and receives a state charter as The Old Woman's Home—a charitable corporation.

1891   Martha Whitworth named first President of the Board of Directors.

c. 1892   Men's Advisory Board formed.

1893   Young Women's Auxiliary formed.

1900   Elizabeth Evert Bellsynder Keith, best known as "Lizzie" becomes President of the Board of Directors.

1906   Discussion begins to secure new property for a larger home to meet the demand of applicants and senior women in need of care.

1907   Lot on West End Avenue purchased and construction for new facility approved.

1908   Groundbreaking ceremony and cornerstone laid for new Old Woman's Home.

1909   Old Woman's Home moves to new location and facility at 2817 West End Avenue bordered by Vanderbilt University and across the street from Centennial Park.

1914–   Endowments established and funds invested by Board of Directors
1917   and Young Women's Auxiliary.

1918   First full time registered nurse, Julia Bentley, hired.

1920   Mary Lanier Cooley Memorial Annex opens to increase residential and health care capacity of OWH.

1920   Residential capacity expands to meet the needs of fifty ladies over the age of sixty-five.

1922   Elizabeth Keith proposes an annex to serve as a home for elderly men.

1923   Keith Memorial Building opens.

1924   Emmy Ewing Keith, daughter-in-law of Lizzie Keith becomes President of the Old Woman's Home.

1931   First couple admitted, Orville and Ida Stief Stockell.

1935   Social Security Act passed by U.S. Congress and signed by President Franklin D. Roosevelt.

c. 1936   Old Woman's Home Chorus established, led and directed by Lorena Armistead Stebbins.

1940   Social Security expanded to include elderly widows and unmarried women, OWH residents first begin receiving Social Security checks, which are turned over to the OWH to offset expenses.

1941   Following the death of Orville Stockell, Board of Directors votes to refocus organizational mission to serve elderly women only.

1942   OWH establishes Sewing Unit for the Red Cross to assist with WWII efforts; Mollie Shook named citywide Sewing Unit Chairman.

1946   Emmy Keith retires as President of the Board of Directors.

1947   First Christmas Party organized by the Young Women's Auxiliary and sponsored by the Board of Directors held at the Maxwell House Hotel.

1958   Resident capacity reaches all-time high with more than seventy senior women living on the West End Avenue campus.

1958   Number of Board members increased to twenty-five; Young Women's Auxiliary renamed Old Woman's Home Auxiliary.

1960   Final Christmas Party held at Maxwell House Hotel before it was destroyed by fire in 1961.

1963   Residential capacity expands to better meet the needs of the home's residents.

1965   Amendment to the Social Security Act of 1935 creates Medicaid and Medicare, passed by the U.S. Congress and signed by President Lyndon B. Johnson leading to another shift in elder health care.

1969   Tax Reform Act passed by U.S. Congress and signed by President Richard M. Nixon designates private, non-profit foundations as charitable organizations, which leads to an expanded nursing home and health services market.

1975   Number of residents declines from an all-time high a decade earlier to approximately forty-five women.

1980   Auxiliary adopts "buddy" system with members paired with residents.

1981   The Old Woman's Home legally changes its name to the West End Home for Ladies.

1981   Decision made to subdivide West End Avenue lot and build new facility on rear plot; older buildings razed and ownership transferred to third-party developer.

1983   Groundbreaking ceremony for new building on Vanderbilt Place.

1984   Residents move to new home located at 2818 Vanderbilt Place on the edge of the campus of Vanderbilt University.

1984   West End Health Care Center opens as a new wing of the Vanderbilt Place facility.

1991   West End Home for Ladies celebrates a century of service with their centennial anniversary.

2000   Resident applications and admissions decline and residents number only twenty-two women over the age of sixty-five.

2001   Board of Directors votes to become a private foundation and legally changes The West End Home for Ladies to The West End Home Foundation.

2001   Board of Directors approves a resolution to halt new admissions to the home.

2002   Revised WEHF constitution and bylaws formally articulates the organization's shift from a residential to a private foundation providing nonresidential services for seniors.

2002   First grant awarded by West End Home Foundation.

2007   Board of Directors votes to merge the budgets of the Board and Auxiliary; Auxiliary dissolved as a formal committee.

2008   Construction of a new wing begins at the Blakeford (private retirement home) after an agreement between WEHF Board and Blakeford executives.

2009   Final nine residents moved into new wing at the Blakeford facility.

2011   Former home at Vanderbilt Place sold to Vanderbilt University.

2013   Lillian Harley, the last resident, passes away.

2014   WEHF launches a website and new logo and shifts exclusively to grantmaking focused on nonprofit agencies serving seniors.

2016   The West End Home Foundation celebrates 125 years of service in Middle Tennessee.

2017   Endowment surpasses $40 million and WEHF continues to enhance its grant program to address the needs of seniors in the impact areas of advocacy, socialization, food/nutrition, healthcare, housing, transportation, wellness, and education.

Appendix A

"The House of Love"
by Will Allen Dromgoole (1909)

We built today this House of Love
For those whose tottering years
Have faced the angry tides of fate
In helplessness and tears

We build for them, "God's poor," whose hands
Their toiling time give o'er
We question not the who nor why
We only know "God's poor."

We know this house of ours must fall,
Our house of hands decay;
But love, that sired the task, will live
When we have passed away.

When stones of crumbled to decay,
And bolts have gathered rust;
And toiling hands and weary feet
Have wandered back to dust.

When pulseless breast beneath the stone,
Lies under pulseless hand,
And time shall toll her changeful years,
Our house of love shall stand.

'Tis not for earthly praise we build,
Nor yet for fame or gold;
But just the blessed privilege,
Of caring for "God's old."

We build in silence, oft in tears,
With loving hands and true;
Who knows if it shall be we've built
Far better than we knew?

'Tis not the cost we count as great,
Nor yet the gracious deed.
But love, that answers "cross the world"
To human creatures need.

No gilded scroll of mighty deeds
These hands of ours may bring.
No written page of glorious things
With which to greet our King.
Yet, who shall say when rolls are called
Of evil and of good.
This gift of ours shall stand like hers,
Who wrought "the best she could."

Who knows the stone our hands brought
For this our house of time,
Shall be the chief foundation stone
To our great hope sublime?

The hope that sees across the years,
The grey of evening skies,
Where fair against the gloom shall flash
The walls of Paradise?

And far beyond the sunset's rim,
Eternal in his sight,
That "house not made with hands" await
Our own soul's rapturous flight?

God take the gift; 'twas ours, 'tis His,
Throughout the untold years;
We dedicate it here today
To God, to Love, to Tears.

God sent the cup our hands have brought
To those who near their goal,
To our last crossing be a cup
Of solace to the soul.

The kindly deed, the cheering hope,
To Age's last lingering sigh,
Smooth our last lonely pillow when
We lay us down to die.

Appendix B

Board of Directors Past Presidents

1892–1900	Martha Whitworth
1900–1924	Elizabeth Evert Bellsynder Keith
1924–1946	Emmie Ewing Keith
1946–1951	Lale L. Murrey
1951–1953	Elizabeth Estes Kirkman
1953–1955	Ellen Lamar Felder Howard
1955–1957	Sarah Shannon Stevenson, Jr.
1957–1959	Frances Carline Stahlman Hunt
1959–1961	Julia Fay Lyon Haun
1961–1963	Martha Killebrew Lanier
1963–1965	Lillian "Tooty" Bradford
1965–1967	Olivia Weaver Boult
1967–1969	Virgina Woolwine Smith
1969–1971	Andrena Butterfield Woodward
1971–1973	Ruth Rodemyer Weaver
1973–1975	Jane Sloan

1975–1977	Adelaide Shull Davis
1977–1979	Susan Warner Bass
1979–1981	Mary Hall "Chippy" Pirtle
1981–1983	Bettye Sue Parrish McNeilly
1983–1985	Annie Laurie Berry
1985–1986	Patricia Kirkman Colton
1987–1988	Anne Parsons
1989–1990	Phyllis Scruggs
1991–1992	Margaret Wiley
1993–1994	Sara Harris Nelson
1995–1996	Ann G. Coleman
1997–1998	Emmie Jackson McDonald
1999–2000	Frances Johnston Earthman
2001–2002	Gayle Elam Smith
2003–2004	Mary Herbert Kelly
2005–2006	Emily Thompson James
2007–2008	Gayle Deerborn Vance
2009–2011	Jean Dobson Farris
2012–2014	Gray Oliver Thornburg
2014–2015	Barbara Cannon-Wall
2015–2016	N. Courtney Hollins
2016–2017	Kim Sumner Hardin

Appendix C

Past Residents (Last Name, Given Name or Spouse's Name)

Aaron	Sarah	Barrett	Mary Elizabeth
Adams	Amanda Sumner	Bateman	Martha H.
Adams	Jennie	Baucom	Annie
Akin	Fannie	Bayless	Delia Francis Buford
Allday	Ella Herman	Bearden	Isola Jane (Jennie)
Allen	Lenah Petri	Beasley	Florence
Allen	Mary Elizabeth	Beasley	Mary Elizabeth
Allen	Myrtle Mae Hill	Beaver	Ruth Lillian Gearhart
Anderson	Julia	Bell	Loula May
Anderson	Marion Foster	Bennett	Maud East Jordan
Anderson	Mattie Willy	Benson	Jennie Kendrick
Anderson	Mildred C. Gatlin	Benson	Lorene May
Andrews	Katie Hollins	Berrying	Augusta
Anglen	Jennie	Bishop	Helen Marr Yerya
Armstrong	Mary Ella Rothrock	Bishop	Maggie Joe
Arnett	Ann Canfield	Black	Erby Lee Sweeney
Arnold	Frances Barrett	Blackburn	Mary Elizabeth
Arnold	Virginia May	Blakeley	Susie M.
Arthur	Nancy M.	Blakely	Annie W. Ewing
Atkins	Virginia Christine	Blitch	Shelley Childress Cabell
Austin	Lula Belle Parker	Bloodworth	Mildred Rebecca
Averitt	Mollie Fite Piper	Bolling	Pauline Ragsdale
Backinstose	B. Florence Rodgers Halsfed	Bomer	Charlene LaRue Shirley
Baird	Shellie Brann	Bond	Harriet Virginia Harper

Bonner	Emma Josephine Hedstrom Spencer	Carr	Mary
Bosworth	Mary A.	Carson	Susan Elizabeth Davis
Bottoms	Agnes Velma	Carter	Katherine H. Lambert
Bowles	Mary	Carver	Mary Jane
Bowles	Ruby Alberta	Cason	Mary
Bowman	Margaret Elizabeth	Cayce	Mary Elizabeth
Boxley	Eva Lois Kindel	Chapman	Ola Jane Kennedy
Boyd	Anna Mai Gwynn (Annie)	Cheairs	Annie Alexander
Boyd	Azile Elizabeth	Childress	Lucy James
Bradford	Martha	Chockley	Frances Anne Parker (Fannie)
Brandau	Susan Seawell	Claiborne	Mary Maxwell (Mollie)
Brandon	Beulah C. Faust	Clark	Elizabeth
Bransford	Mary Bowles	Clark	Jennie Mae
Brittin	Lillie Crutcher	Clayton	Lillian May Driver
Brooks	Emma Moss Adams	Cochran	Valeria Wheeler
Brown	Anna E.	Cockrill	Sallie Louise
Brown	Mary Elizabeth Wolfe	Coffman	Mrs.
Buchanan	Pocahontas	Coldren	Lula Cox
Buford	Madeline Boyd Hall (Mattie)	Coleman	Mary Ann (Mollie)
Bullard	Marcella D. Carney	Collier	Eva Douglas
Burchfield	Lelia Jane	Collins	Clara Virginia
Burchitt	Elizabeth	Collins	Nannie Williams
Burkitt	Bessie Fly Austin	Comingore	Charity Stagg
Burks	Montie Marie	Cook	Martha Washington
Burnett	Maggie	Cook	Nora Alice Campbell
Burney	Annie C.	Cook	Sarah Bentley
Bush	Mada Edna Rogers	Corbett	Barbara
Cage	Priscilla Douglas	Corum	Frances Stratton
Cannon	Nellie Robertson	Cowles	Elizabeth Shute
Cantrell	Lillian Bragg	Cox	Emma Minchin
Caperton	Mary Jane (Mollie)	Crawford	Ellen
Cardwell	Anne Wilson	Crawford	Mary
Carpenter	Pauline	Crawford	Ruby Ross
Carr	Catherine	Crockett	Annie Childress
		Crockett	Lillian James

Cruchfield	Louise		Featherston	Armatine Smith
Currey	Elizabeth McCarthy		Feldhaus	Clara Pauline
Dail	Rosa Amy		Fisher	Anna Hawkins
Davis	Anna Washington Stretch		Fitzhugh	Bertha H. Riddile
Davis	Emma P.		Fitzhugh	Cora Elizabeth Haley Green
Davis	Josephine		Flippen	Fannie Allison Anderson
Davis	Mary Anne		Ford	Emma
Davis	Sarah Frances		Forde	Elizabeth
Dean	Ellen Elizabeth McGuff		Foreman	Lucy A.
Dilahunty	Mary T.		Fort	Della Dancey
Dingess	Ida Hildred		Foy	Johnnie Louise Francis Laseter
Doss	Velma C.		Franklin	Georgiana Lee
Dowe	Eloise Eakin		Frayser	Annie E.
Downing	Callie McGuire		Frierson	Stella
Drake	Adah B. Crump		Fuqua	Martha Stewart Laurent
Driver	Mrs.			(Marie)
Duffy	Nell Cannon Satterwhite		Gaines	Ala Lewis
Duggan	Hester Caroline Elliott		Garrett	Audrey Cannon
Duling	Kitty Riley		Gatlin	Katie Lou
Dunn	Katherine (Kate)		Gattinger	Augusta (Gussie)
Dunnivant	Mattie		Gilbert	Valeria Rose
Eatherly	Ethel Doolin		Gill	Nannie
Edmundson	Katherine Quintard		Ginn	Ellen Jane Douglas Jones
Edwards	Maggie Clay		Glasgow	Eliza
Eggleston	Eleanor		Gleaves	Jessie Florence
Elliot	Julia		Glenn	Kate Virginia
Ellis	Agnes		Gordon	Martha M.
Ellis	Elizabeth		Graham	Annie Mary Althauser
Emerson	Hetty McEwen		Gray	Margaret Amanda (Maggie)
Eubanks	Olivia		Green	Mrs.
Ewing	Carrie		Green	Ollie Elmer
Ewing	Ellen McGavock		Greer	Marietta Rowland
Falconnet	Mary Carolyn		Gresham	Rebecca Ann
Farr	Mary Helen Helm		Gribble	Flora Louise
Farrell	Mamie Kuhn		Grimmett	Mary Elizabeth

Grooms	Sarah V.	Hill	Nancye Benton
Guill	Elizabeth Miles (Bessie)	Hilliard	Mary Green Palmer
Haggard	Mary Wilton Craig	Hinkle	Anna T.
Hale	Edith Mae	Hinton	Elizabeth Augusta Lathrope
Hall	Birdie Rebecca Reid	Hix	Marion Eleanor Jordan
Hall	Evelyn Cartwright	Hobbs	Louise Gatlin
Hall	Florence	Hockaday	Anna Lee Baxter
Hall	Mrs. L.B. Hale	Hoes	Josephine Walker Pemberton
Hall	Luella Houze (Lula)	Holliday	Ruth T.
Hall	Mary Ann	Hollins	Carrie
Hall	Pearl Nineva Cornwell	Holt	Amelia Shoffner Wirsching
Hamby	Jimmie Lavinia	Holt	Dulcenia Reaves (Della)
Hardaway	Kate V.	House	Tabitha
Hardison	Katherine Young	Houser	Mattie Elizabeth Thomas
Hardy	Annie Mary	Houston	Belle McAlister
Harley	Lillian Mina	Huckaby	Cora Bell Roberts
Harper	Frances Rebecca Harrison	Hudgins	Annie Todd
Harris	Mrs.	Hughes	Imelda
Harris	Mrs. R. S.	Hunt	Martha Jane
Harris	Virginia Williams	Hunter	Myrtle Dean
Harrison	Catherine G.	Hutchinson	Lizzie Burt Dobbs Young
Harrison	Kate L. Matlock	Ireland	Mattie Arnold
Harrison	Lucille Dolan	Jaccard	Louise
Hart	`Effie May Perkins	Jackson	Carrye Ruffin
Harvill	Minna Hill Haynes	Jennings	Jane Belle
Haughton	Lucy Gill	Jennings	Mary
Hays	Frances Elizabeth (Fannie)	Johns	Bessie Young
Hays	Ninnie Imojean Warmath	Johnson	Fannie W.
Head	Ann Wharton	Johnson	Mary E. Chamberlain
Hendley	Jimmie	Jones	Clemmie Atkins
Henry	Caroline Owen	Jones	Gertrude E. Hodges
Hereford	Jennie Mai Sellers	Jones	Hattie Corrille McClellan
Herrin	Ruby Lee Young	Jones	Medora
Hersh	Eleanor May Herts	Jones	Roberta Brownlee
Hester	Cornelia Hayes	Jones	Sally

Jones	Tillie Miles
Jordan	M. Francis Cordie
Kallock	Cora A. Payne
Keith	Mary McCullough (Culla)
Kelley	Anita Parker
Kelley	Josie
Kercheval	Margaretta McEwen
Kern	Clara Belle Boggs
King	Muriel C.
King	Rebecca W.
Kitch	Mattie
Kittenger	Kate
Kittinger	Jane Garmen
Knox	Katherine Christine
Kumpf	Martha Jessica Martyne (Mattie)
Kyle	Henrietta Warren Keohm
Kyle	Ida
LeSueur	Katherine Margaret
Lampley	Ethel Carneal
Landon	Blanche
Lanier	Daisy Earl
Lavender	Nancy
Lawrence	Anna C. Staub
Legler	Edith Alice Dall
Leslie	Mrs. J. D.
Lester	Aileen Bainbridge
Lester	Carrie
Lewis	Lena Hutton
Lewis	Nancy E.
Lilly	Evalena Rozella Haggard
Lipscomb	Minna Lee Scott (Minnie)
Little	Eva Butts
Little	M. E.
Livingston	Letitia Pruett
Lovell	Willie Mai
Luckey	Martha M. Lee
Lunn	Mrs.
McAdams	Emily J.
McBryde	Martha Leonard
McClure	Fannie Mai
McComb	Charlie Dickinson
McCormack	Margaret (Maggie)
McDaniel	Laura Lucy Terry
McGlothlin	Lillian Ferrell
McGoodwin	Francis Bryan (Fannie)
McGriff	Hettie M. Gribble
McIntyre	Anna Marie Thoni
McKee	Mrs. Jonathon Miller
McNish	Ruth Mai Deal
Malone	Laura
Manning	Gertrude
March	Sallie
Marlin	Sadie Ida
Martin	Bettye
Martin	Emily Hayes
Martin	Moselle Florence
Massey	Aneska Dodge
Massey	Lucille Baugh
Mathes	Nancy
Matthews	Mrs.
Matthews	Tennessee Elizabeth Brown
May	Hattie Douglas
Mayberry	Elizabeth
Meals	Fred Lucille Ferrell
Merrill	Lura Ann
Miles	Lida Whiteside
Miller	Caroline
Miller	Edith Free
Milligan	Mary Worthington

Minor	Jennie Martin
Moody	Sallie Clay Martin Tillman Cannon
Mooney	Grace Reubelt
Moore	Florence Williams
Moore	Isabella
Moore	Lera Bush
Moore	Marion Elizabeth Cole (Bettye)
Morrissey	Frances Amanda Brown
Morton	Mrs.
Moseley	Nora D. Byrn
Mullendore	Lucille Bruce
Murdock	Belle Green
Murphy	Laura Carney
Murrey	Anne Elizabeth Rankin Osborne
Neely	Cora Etta
Nevins	Ellen Malone (Nellie)
Newby	Mollie
Nicholson	Maria L.
Niles	Mary H. Dismukes
Northern	Joe Bennett
Oman	Jessie Elizabeth Murdock
Oman	Mary Daisy Booth
Osteen	Dorothy Ellen Lish
Owen	Anna
Owen	Francis Hilda Slayden
Owen	Nannie Ferriss
Palmer	Anna Allen
Parham	Dora
Parker	Mary Lanier
Parrish	Elizabeth Coyle
Parrish	Minnie Rebecca Lee
Passmore	Emma H.

Patterson	Mrs.
Patterson	Mary Patty Oliver
Patterson	Sue Rippy
Payne	Maude
Pearcy	Mary
Pearson	Josephine A.
Pennington	Emaline Waller
Percel	Judith
Peterson	Julia Erickson
Phillips	Brenda Bell
Pickard	Harriet
Pierce	Margaret
Pike	Minnie Marie Khone
Pike	Sallie
Pitts	Cora
Polk	Minnie Todd
Potter	Ruth Adams
Powell	Rene Webster
Pritchard	DeLosse Balfour
Proctor	Jennelle Porter
Purnell	Pattie
Randolph	Nancy Williams
Rankin	Ophelia Barham
Ranson	Mary Guerrant Bibb
Rauscher	Wynona Covington
Rawls	Martha Thomas
Reid	Lou Sherrill
Rhodes	Martha Ann Howington Stewart
Rich	Mary Frances Locke
Richardson	Anne
Richardson	Annella Smith
Ridings	Francis
Riggan	Adelia
Riggan	Lizzie Henry

Riley	Susan Elsie Morrison		Smith	Kate
Ringpfeil	Mary Madelina Vollmer		Smith	Mary
Ritter	Maud Menees Smalling		Smith	Mary Frances Starr
Roberts	Orelia Jones		Smith	Rosalyn Critser
Robertson	Laura Brown		Snead	Ama Irene
Robertson	Martha M. Schmitt		Snead	Lula Estelle
Rohde	Bertha Mai Brown		Snodgrass	Rosa Maude
Rose	Katherine Perkins (Katye)		Snow	Elizabeth
Rudolph	Mary		Speer	Abigail Fuller Willimarter
Rutland	Fannie McCulley		Spire	Lottie
Scales	Mary Ellis		Stebbins	Lorena Hydinger Armistead
Schluter	Mattie A.		Stegall	Florence Magnolia Batey
Searcy	Elizabeth Mary		Stephens	Jennie King
Searle	Mary Emma Norman		Stephenson	Oda Riley
Shadion	Ruby Hill		Stevens	Annie Hubbard
Sharpe	Tennie Boyd Coleman		Stewart	Lelah Thomas
Shaw	Annie Rai Doyle		Stivers	Willie Mae Huddleston (Billie)
Shaw	Fannie			
Shearin	Nannie		Stockell	Ida Gover Steif
Shields	Mary		Stockell	Orville Ewing
Shields	Susie Gray		Stone	Harriett Warden
Shipp	Albert William		Strong	Louise Thompson
Shipp	Lily Rountree		Stuart	Belle W.
Shockley	Mary Theresa		Sullivan	Mary Leanora Clark
Shook	Mollie Wright		Summitt	Elizabeth Mae Hilliard
Short	Wilma Louise		Swearington	Edna Kelsey
Simrall	Elizabeth Douglas (Libbie)		Sweeney	Josephine Brashear (Jo)
Sinclair	Eva Alene Travis		Talbot	Harriet
Skaggs	Emma Harry		Tamble	Hetty Joseph
Sloan	Lillie Locken		Tavel	Hellen
Sloan	Martha		Tavel	Isabel
Smiley	Penelope Eliza (Pennie)		Tavel	Pauline Mary
Smith	Caroline Lucille Cox		Taylor	Alyne Alice
Smith	Daisy Lucille		Taylor	Lavinia
Smith	Eliza Jane Roope (Jennie)		Thompson	Clara Bryant

Thompson	Fannie Martin	White	Annie Louise West
Thompson	Iola Delores Tooke Perry	White	Marilyn Chisholm
Thompson	Viola M. Brinkley Pulliam	White	Nora E. Frank
Towns	Lela Barber	Wilkins	Mary Charlotte
Trabue	Lena Wilhoite	Wilkinson	Roberta
Trotter	Annie Myrtle Manley	Williams	Cora McClure
Trotter	Beulah Beatrice	Williams	Eddine Guill
Tucker	Frances Elizabeth Dean	Williams	Eudora Hardeman
Tucker	Tennie	Williams	Florence Taylor
Tulloss	Daisy Cleveland	Williams	Jennie
Turner	Katie Louise	Willis	Allie Shivers
Turner	Louise Alice Faust	Willson	Mary F. Stapp
Turner	Mary E.	Willy	Mr.
Tuthill	Mary Dolph	Willy	Mrs.
Tyer	Mary Hall	Wilson	Tennie
Van	Mrs.	Winbourn	Ella Bell
Wadley	Effie	Winfrey	Lillian Eugene Easley
Walker	Armilda Turner Hill	Wood	Alta Hula Walters
Wallace	Ada May Cleveland	Worke	Julia
Walton	Sarah	Worley	Lela Young
Warfield	Mary Vollie Alwell	Wray	Mrs. W. A.
Warfield	Minnie Bell Johnson	Wyman	Isabel W. Beedy
Warren	Ella M.	Yarbrough	Elizabeth Ann McClean
Warren	Sallie A.	Young	Emma Haynie
Washington	Katherine Ellen	Young	Nell Jane Powell
Watson	Cora Elizabeth		
Watson	Florence		
Weakley	Sallie		
Weaver	Minnie Bacon		
Webster	Isadora Maltby (Iana)		
Weddington	Leila Liles		
Welburn	Maude Bush		
Welch	Mary Pauline Ray		
Westenberger	Mary C. Hutchison		
Wheeless	McAlister		

Appendix D

Endowed Room Inscriptions

ENDOWED BY
MR. GEORGE STOCKELL
IN MEMORY OF
HIS MOTHER

ENDOWED BY
MRS. J. S. REEVES
1909

CORNERSTONE BOX
FROM "OLD WOMAN'S HOME"
2817 WEST END AVE.
1908

IN MEMORY OF
MRS. EMMA CLAIBORNE CHAMPE
1846-1911

ENDOWED BY
MRS. L. H. LANIER
1891

IN LOVING MEMORY OF
MARY ELIZA TREANOR
BY HER DAUGHTER
NELLIE TREANOR STOKES

IN MEMORY OF
DELLA FORD CALLENDER
FURNISHED BY
MRS. ALEX S. CALDWELL

ENDOWED BY
MISS STELLA FRIERSON
1919

ENDOWED 1910 BY
MISS NANNIE M. JACKSON
IN MEMORY
OF HER MOTHER

ENDOWED BY
NELLIE ROBERTSON CANNON
IN MEMORY OF HER SON
PEYTON ROBERTSON CANNON

ENDOWED BY
LILLIE R. SHIPP
IN MEMORY OF HER HUSBAND
ALBERT W. SHIPP

ENDOWED IN MEMORY OF
HENRY TANDY ARNOLD
BY HIS DAUGHTER
MATTIE A. IRELAND

ENDOWED IN MEMORY OF
DR. WILL F. ARNOLD - U.S.N.
BY HIS SISTER
FRANCIS B. ARNOLD

ENDOWED BY
MRS. MARY BELLE KEITH MADDIN
IN MEMORY OF HER FATHER AND MOTHER
MR. AND MRS. SAMUEL J. KEITH

ENDOWED IN LOVING MEMORY OF
JULIA N. MORE
BY HER SON
E. LIVINGFIELD MORE

ENDOWED BY
CORA PAYNE KALLOCK
IN MEMORY OF HER HUSBAND
ALBERT ROYAL KALLOCK

ENDOWED BY
MAUDE M. PAYNE
IN MEMORY OF HER SISTER
ANNA PAYNE

CHEEK DINING ROOM
IN GRATEFUL APPRECIATION FOR THE
MANY YEARS OF DEDICATED SERVICES OF
ROBERT STANLEY CHEEK
AND
HELEN PICKSLAY CHEEK
1975

ENDOWED BY
MRS. MAMIE WILSON HILL
IN MEMORY OF HER MOTHER
MRS. FRANCES BUTTERWORTH WILSON
AND HER AUNT
MISS MARY LELIA BUTTERWORTH
"BLESSED ARE THE PURE IN HEART
FOR THEY SHALL SEE GOD"

IN LOVING MEMORY OF
MR. AND MRS. WALTER KEITH
AND THEIR GENEROUS
WORK FOR THIS HOME

KEITH WING
1956
REPLACES THE BUILDING PRESENTED
IN 1925 BY
MRS. SAMUEL J. KEITH
IN MEMORY OF HER HUSBAND

IN LOVING MEMORY OF
FRANCES STAHLMAN HUNT
AND
ELLEN FELDER HOWARD STEMPFEL

ENDOWED BY
MINA MUTH MILLER
IN LOVING MEMORY OF HER MOTHER
EMILE AMENDE MUTH

IN LOVING MEMORY OF
ROBERT MOORE CONDRA
OUR STEADFAST FRIEND
1989

IN LOVING MEMORY
OF
CORRINNE CRAIG PARRISH
1986

IN HONOR OF
DUDLEY C. FORT
FOR HIS GENEROUS CONTRIBUTIONS
TO THE WEST END
HOME FOR LADIES

IN MEMORY OF
ANNIE LAURIE AND
FRANK CARL STAHLMAN

IN LOVING MEMORY OF
ANN POTTER WILSON
1986

IN LOVING MEMORY OF
ELIZABETH SUDEKUM
JOHNSTON
1988

NATHAN CORNELIUS CRAIG
IN MEMORY OF
MY MOTHER
MAMIE CROCKETT CRAIG
1969

WINSTON BRIGHT THOMAS
IN MEMORY OF HIS MOTHER
MARY BRIGHT THOMAS

COOLEY BUILDING
MARY LANIER COOLEY MEMORIAL
BY HER SON
JULIAN S. COOLEY
1914

IN LOVING MEMORY OF
MY MOTHER
EMMA KEMPKAU

—————

CLARA A. KEMPKAU

ENDOWED BY
MRS. ANDREW PRICE
IN LOVING MEMORY OF
HER MOTHER
MRS. LAVINIA HYNES GAY
"BLEST BE THE TIE THAT BINDS
OUR HEARTS IN CHRISTIAN LOVE"

ENDOWED IN MEMORY OF
MR. & MRS. HENRY HOUZE
BY THEIR DAUGHTER
LOUELLA HOUZE HALL

ENDOWED BY
MR. GEORGE STOCKELL
IN MEMORY OF
HIS MOTHER

ENDOWED BY
MRS. VALREIA ROSE GILBERT
IN MEMORY OF HER SISTER
MISS TENNIE ROSE
ENDOWED BY
MRS. FLORENCE TAYLOR WILLIAMS

GRACE, MERCY AND PEACE
TO YOU
ENDOWED 1891 BY
DR. AND MRS. WM. MORROW
ENDOWED BY
MRS. EMMA HAYNIE YOUNG

ROOM GIVEN IN
MEMORY OF
MRS. HORACE HILL
GIVEN BY
FRANCES HILL CALDWELL

ENDOWED BY
MISS MARY MILLER
1845-1916
"BLESSED ARE THE
PURE IN HEART"

ENDOWED BY
MRS. B. F. WILSON
AS A MEMORIAL TO
HER MOTHER
"THE LIGHT OF HER LOVE
STILL BRIGHTENS THE WAY"

ENDOWED BY
MRS. LIZZIE McGRIFF DEAN
IN MEMORY OF HER HUSBAND
JAMES WILLIAM DEAN

ENDOWED BY
MISS ANNA C. HENKEL
1904

ENDOWED IN MEMORY OF
CHARLES E. HALL
BY HIS WIFE
LUELLA HOUZE HALL

ENDOWED BY
MRS. JOHN MILLER McKEE
1909

TO HONOR
MRS. WALTER STOKES
TREASURER FOR 29 YEARS

ENDOWED BY
CHARLES N. BUFORD
1921

IN MEMORY
OF
MARTHA S. TILLMAN

IN MEMORIAM
—————
MEDORA BROWN DORTCH
1833-1902

ENDOWED 1891 BY
MR. AND MRS. S.J. KEITH
IN MEMORY OF
BIRDIE KEITH

ROOM GIVEN IN
MEMORY OF
DR. AND MRS. McPHEETERS GLASGOW
GIVEN BY THEIR CHILDREN
McPHEETERS GLASGOW , JR.: MARY BELLE GAMBILL:
MARGART STANFORD: KEITH LAUDERDALE:
ELIZABETH PHILLIPS: AND GRACE ELLEN WATKINS

ROOM GIVEN
IN MEMORY OF
FLORENCE MOSS WILSON
GIVEN BY
ANN AND DAVID K. WILSON

ROOM GIVEN
IN MEMORY OF
NELLIE TREANOR STOKES
GIVEN BY
ELLEN STOKES WEMYSS

ROOM GIVEN
IN MEMORY OF
FRANCES STAHLMAN HUNT
AND ANNIE LAURIE STAHLMAN

Endnotes

Chapter 1

1   Eliza Crosthwaite was born in 1843 in Lawrence County, Tennessee.

2   Newspaper clipping, *Nashville Daily American*, n.p. 1887, *West End Home Foundation Collection*, Metropolitan Nashville Archives.

3   Carole Haber and Brian Gratton, *Old Age and the Search for Security* (New York: Cambridge University Press, 1994), 130.

4   Carole Haber, "Nursing Homes: History," Available online: http://medicine.jrank.org/pages/1243/Nursing-Homes-History.html.

5   Jeannette Sloan Warner, *An Informal History of the Auxiliary to the Board of the Old Woman's Home* (Nashville: privately printed by Old Women's Home, 1960), *West End Home Foundation Collection*, Metropolitan Nashville Archives.

6   Mrs. J.L. Watkins, "Nashville's Old Woman's Home: Its Founding and Its History," newspaper clipping, c. 1918.

7   Haverford College Library, Haverford, PA, Quaker Collection, Caleb Cope and Family Papers. Available Online: http://hdl.library.upenn.edu/1017/d/pacscl/HAVERFORD_HC1222USPHC.

8   Memucan Hunt Howard, *Recollections of Tennessee* (Nashville: Tennessee Historical Society, 1883), n.p. Available online: http://www.tnyesterday.com/yesterday_henderson/recolltn.html

9   W. Woodford Clayton, *History of Davidson County, Tennessee, with Illustrations and Biographical Sketches of its Prominent Men and Pioneers* (Philadelphia: J. W. Lewis & Co., 1880), 249–53.

10 Memucan Hunt Howard, *Recollections of Tennessee*, n.p.

11 "Watkins Institute," *Annual Report of the State Superintendent of Public Instruction for Tennessee, 1899* (Nashville: Foster & Webb Printers, 1899), 246. Available online: http://bit.ly/2hOMdxa

12 Excerpt of Mr. M. H. Howard Last Will and Testament, *West End Home Foundation Collection*, Metropolitan Nashville Archives.

13 Ibid.

14 "Home for the Aged Women and Orphan Waifs," n.a., n.p., 1887, *West End Home Foundation Collection*, Metropolitan Nashville Archives. The document continues, "We have the assurance of the trustees of the Howard fund that if we raise and additional $1200.00 they will turn funds over to the Home." It should be noted that $100 in the 1880s would be more than $2,000 in 2016.

15 Paul H. Bergeron, Stephen V. Ash, Jeanette Keith, *Tennesseans and Their History* (Knoxville: University of Tennessee Press, 1999), 214.

16 Mrs. J. L. Watkins, "Nashville's Old Woman's Home: Its Founding and Its History," newspaper clipping, c. 1918.

17 Meeting Minutes, January 19, 1892, *West End Home Foundation Collection*, Metropolitan Nashville Archives.

18 Frank P. Hume, "Along Old Cherry Street," 1912, Reprinted in "Nashville History," (2010), http://nashvillehistory.blogspot.com/2010/12/along-old-cherry-street.html.

19 For more on William Walker see: Ron Soodalter, "William Walker: King of the 19th Century Filibuster," March 4, 2010, http://www.historynet.com/. Walker was ultimately captured and killed by firing squad in Nicauraga.

20 Meeting Minutes, June 1892, *West End Home Foundation Collection*, Metropolitan Nashville Archives.

21 Annual Report of the Old Woman's Home, 1897, newspaper clipping, *West End Home Foundation Collection*, Metropolitan Nashville Archives.

22 "Old Woman's Home: Closes Successful Year Free From Debt," *Nashville American*, 1906.

23 Ibid.

24 Ridley Wills II, Interview by author, January 11, 2017, Nashville, Tennessee.

25 Old Woman's Home Scrapbook, 1906, *West End Home Foundation Collection*, Metropolitan Nashville Archives.

26 "Cheatham et al. v. Nashville Trust Co. et al," *Southwestern Reporter* 57 (June-July 1900), 202–05. Available online: https://books.google.com/. Susan McGavock Smith died in 1894, the OWH attempted to liquidate her bequest in 1899, which prompted the lawsuit by some of her heirs claiming that the organization's trustee structure had changed, as the original charter had only been signed by men (mostly spouses of Board of Director members), and was therefore void. The court sided with the OWH.

27 Newspaper clipping, 1908 (WEHF Scrapbook, 1910), *West End Home Foundation Collection*, Metropolitan Nashville Archives. Sara Ward Conley was the great aunt of Jean Ward

Oldfield and the sister of Dr. William E. Ward who founded Ward Seminary with his wife, Eliza Hudson Ward, in 1865.

28 Newspaper clipping, 1908 (WEHF Scrapbook, 1910), *West End Home Foundation Collection*, Metropolitan Nashville Archives.

29 "Will Allen Dromgoole (1860–1934)," *The Poetry Foundation* (2017), Accessible online: https://www.poetryfoundation.org/poems-and-poets/poets/detail/will-allen-dromgoole.

30 "Cornerstone of New Building Laid," *Nashville American*, 1908 (WEHF Scrapbook, 1910), *West End Home Foundation Collection*, Metropolitan Nashville Archives.

31 WEHF Scrapbook, 1910, *West End Home Foundation Collection*, Metropolitan Nashville Archives.

32 "Remove To-Day to New Home: Change of Quarters of Old Woman's Home, New Memorial Endowments," newspaper clipping, WEHF Scrapbook, 1908–1921, *West End Home Foundation Collection*, Metropolitan Nashville Archives.

33 Ibid.

34 "Benefit Tea Is Success," *Nashville Banner*, newspaper clipping, 1919.

35 "Annual Report of Old Woman's Home," *Nashville Banner*, newspaper clipping, 1918.

36 Ibid.

37 Ibid.

38 Mrs. J.L. Watkins, "Nashville's Old Woman's Home: Its Founding and Its History," newspaper clipping, c. 1918. Mrs. Watkins was the Board of Directors Secretary.

39 Ibid.

40 Mrs. J.L. Watkins, "The Twenty-Ninth Annual Report of the Old Woman's Home," 1920, *West End Home Foundation Collection*, Metropolitan Nashville Archives.

41 "Old Woman's Home: Closes Successful Year Free From Debt," *Nashville American*, newspaper clipping, 1906, *West End Home Foundation Collection*, Metropolitan Nashville Archives.

42 The Massachusetts State Legislature called such women the "worthy old" of society in 1910.

Chapter 2

1 Walter Keith, letter to West End Home for Ladies Board of Directors, 1984, *West End Home Collection*, Metropolitan Nashville Archives.

2 *Who's Who in Tennessee: A Biographical Reference Book of Notable Tennesseans of To-Day.* (Memphis: Paul & Douglas Co, 1911). The entry in *Who's Who in Tennessee* continues:

Percy D. Maddin was an attorney for the Fourth National Bank of Nashville
and of Louisville & Nashville Railway Company for fifteen years; Vice-President
Tennessee State Bar Association 1909–10; President 1910–11; member American
Bar Association; several years member of its council for Tennessee; Director Fourth
National Bank for seventeen years; Director of Nashville & Decatur Railroad;
Professor of Law in Vanderbilt University since 1900; member of K. of P., Masons,
Hermitage Club and Nashville Golf and Country Club, Phi Delta Theta fraternity
and Phi Beta Kappa of Vanderbilt University; President McKendree M. E. Church,
South, Corporation, and Chairman of its Board of Stewards; also President of
Galloway Memorial Hospital.

3   "Annual Report of Old Woman's Home Shows Work Carried on Creditably," *Nashville Banner*, February 8, 1924.

4   Walter Keith, letter to West End Home for Ladies Board of Directors, 1984, *West End Home Collection*, Metropolitan Nashville Archives.

5   Letter from Percy D. Maddin to the Board of Directors, 1922, *West End Home Collection*, Metropolitan Nashville Archives.

6   Ibid.

7   Cindy Dickinson, Interview by author, December 22, 2016, Nashville, Tennessee.

8   "James C. McReynolds," Chicago-Kent College of Law at Illinois Tech, *Oyez*. Available online: https://www.oyez.org/justices/james_c_mcreynolds.

9   WEHF Scrapbook 1908, *West End Home Collection*, Metropolitan Nashville Archives.

10   "Old Woman's Home Make Thirty-Third Annual Report," *Nashville Banner*, 1923.

11   Ibid.

12   Ibid.

13   Ibid.

14   Don Doyle, *Nashville in the New South, 1880–1930* (Knoxville: University of Tennessee Press, 1985), 217.

15   Ibid., 230.

16   Robert Margo, "Employment and Unemployment in the 1930s," *Journal of Economic Perspectives* 7 (Spring 1993), 41.

17   "New Officers Elected," *Nashville Banner*, 1918.

18   Jeannette Sloan Warner, *An Informal History of the Auxiliary to the Board of the Old Woman's Home* (Nashville: privately printed by Old Women's Home, 1960), *West End Home*

Foundation Collection, Metropolitan Nashville Archives.

19 "Program Given for Old Woman's Home," *Tennessean*, December 7, 1932.

20 "Successful Year is Shown in Old Woman's Home Report" *Nashville Banner*, February 4, 1930.

21 "The Social Security Act of 1935," *Social Security Administration*, https://www.ssa.gov/history/35act.html.

22 Carole Haber and Brian Gratton, *Old Age and the Search for Security* (New York: Cambridge University Press, 1994), 152.

23 Graham D. Rowles, Pamela B. Teaster, *Long-Term Care in an Aging Society: Theory and Practice* (New York: Spring Publishing, 2016), 51.

24 Ibid.

25 Martha McSteen, "Fifty Years of Social Security," *Social Security Bulletin*, 48 (August 1985), 38–39.

26 Ida May Fuller lived until 1975 and passed away just months before her 101th birthday.

27 Nancy J. Altman, *The Battle for Social Security: From FDR's Vision to Bush's Gamble* (Hoboken, NJ: John Wiley & Sons, 2005), 137–49.

28 McSteen, "Fifty Years of Social Security," 39-40.

29 "The Roosevelts Visit Nashville," Nashville Public Library "Off the Shelf Series." Available online: http://nashvillepubliclibrary.org, November 2014.

30 Eleanor Roosevelt, "My Day, October 6, 1938," *The Eleanor Roosevelt Papers Digital Edition* (2008). Available online: https://www2.gwu.edu/~erpapers/myday/displaydoc.cfm?_y=1938&_f=md055077.

31 WEHF Scrapbook, c. 1950. *West End Home Collection*, Metropolitan Nashville Archives.

32 Robert Guy Spinney, *World War II in Nashville: Transformation of the Homefront* (Knoxville: University of Tennessee Press, 1998), 117–18.

33 Ibid., 119.

34 Ibid.

35 "Give Three Cheers," *Tennessean*, March 1945, 8.

36 Newspaper clipping, *Nashville Banner*, February 1928, *West End Home Collection*, Metropolitan Nashville Archives.

37 "They Will Be Remembered," *Nashville Banner*, May 11, 1942.

38 Ibid.

39 "Letter to the Editor," May 15, 1941, *Tennessean*.

40   "Letter to the Editor," May 17, 1941, *Tennessean.*

41   "Mrs. Emmy Ewing Keith," *Tennessean*, December 16, 1951.

42   "Old Woman's Home Holds Board Meeting," newspaper clipping, 1948, *West End Home Collection*, Metropolitan Nashville Archives.

43   "Annual Report of Old Woman's Home Shows Work Carried on Creditably" *Nashville Banner*, February 8, 1924.

44   Ibid.

45   *Nashville Banner*, December 20, 1951.

46   Ibid.

47   "Ladies of 80 See Santa," *Nashville Banner*, December 17, 1952.

48   "Christmas Party Guests Escorted," *Nashville Banner*, December 1952.

49   Ibid.

50   The article states, "Cleverly arranged honor guests were 'blind dates' of local business and civic leaders. John Teas escorted Rosa Dail and John Sloan was with Sadie Marlin."

51   *Nashville Tennessean*, December 19, 1952.

52   Ibid.

53   "Santa Visit Girls Age 68 and Up," *Nashville Tennessean*, December 1954.

54   Ibid.

55   "Christmas Party Guests Escorted," *Nashville Banner*, December 1952.

56   "Santa Visit Girls Age 68 and Up," *Nashville Tennessean*, December 1954.

57   Ibid.

58   Ibid.

59   "Christmas Party Guests Escorted," *Nashville Banner*, December 1952.

60   "Ladies of 80 See Santa," *Nashville Banner*, December 17, 1952.
     "Christmas Party Guests Escorted," *Nashville Banner*, December 1952.

61   "Santa Visit Girls Age 68 and Up," *Nashville Tennessean*, December 1954.

62   *Nashville Banner*, December 20, 1951.

Chapter 3

1   "Old Woman's Home Marks Its 50th Year on Thursday," *Nashville Tennessean*, October 5, 1958.

2   WEHF Scrapbook, c. 1960, *West End Home Collection*, Metropolitan Nashville Archives.

3   Carole Haber, "Nursing Homes: History," Available online: http://medicine.jrank.

org/pages/1243/Nursing-Homes-History.html.

4   Ibid.

5   Paul Arnsberger, Melissa Ludlum, Margaret Riley, and Mark Shannon, "A History of the Tax-Exempt Sector: An SOI Perspective, *Statistics of Income Bulletin* (Winter 2008), 107–10.

6   Peter Dobkin Hall, *Inventing the Nonprofit Sector and Other Essays on Philanthropy, Voluntarism, and Nonprofit Organizations* (Baltimore: John Hopkins Press, 1992), 19.

7   OWH Constitution and Bylaws, Nashville, Tennessee, 1940, 2, *West End Home Collection*, Metropolitan Nashville Archives.

8   For more see: Herbert H. Slatery, *Tennessee's New Non-Profit Corporation Act: A Flexible and Modern Statutory Approach* (Nashville: M. Lee Smith, 1987).

9   "Old Woman's Home Marks Its 50th Year on Thursday," *Nashville Tennessean*, October 5, 1958.

10 Anne Coleman, Interview with Grace Awh, Nashville Tennessee, June 11, 2014, *West End Home Collection*, Metropolitan Nashville Archives.

11 OWH Constitution and Bylaws, Nashville, Tennessee, 1958, 3.

12 Ibid., 6.

13 OWH Constitution and Bylaws, Nashville, Tennessee, 1990, 5.

14 "Lillie Morrow Anderson," *Nashville Tennessean*, February 19, 1957.

15 "Charles R. Clements," *Tennessean*, June 1, 1960.

16 "Lillian Scott Neel," *Tennessean*, April 14, 1966.

17 "Emmy Keith Jackson," *Tennessean*, April 30, 1973.

18 Cindy Dickinson, interview by author, March 2, 2017, Nashville, Tennessee.

19 "Helen Louise Pickslay Cheek," *Tennessean*, September 23, 1975.

20 Carole Nelson, interview by author, January 17, 2017. *Third National Bank v. Hall* (1948). Available online: https://casetext.com/case/third-nat-bank-v-hall.

21 "Hortense Bigelow Ingram," *Tennessean*, September 29, 1979.

22 Patricia Ingram Hart, interview with author, Nashville, Tennessee, February 28, 2017.

23 "Margaret Warner White," *Tennessean*, October 20, 1981.

24 OWH Constitution and Bylaws, Nashville, Tennessee, 1958.

25 "Mabel Lyon," *Tennessean*, May 30, 1956.

26 Anita Frazer was a member of the Tennessee Historical Society, Colonial Dames, Daughters of the Revolution, Children's Museum, American Red Cross, Garden Club, Junior League of Nashville. She also served as president of the Centennial Club and Nashville Museum of Art.

27   "Annual Report of Old Woman's Home Shows Work Carried on Creditably" *Nashville Banner*, February 8, 1924.

28   "Old Woman's Home Marks Its 50th Year on Thursday," *Nashville Tennessean*, October 5, 1958.

29   "Nails Exclusively by Salt and Pepper," *Tennessean*, September 21, 1995.

30   Cemele Richardson, interview with Anne Morgan, Nashville, Tennessee, June 11, 2014, *West End Home Collection*, Metropolitan Nashville Archives.

31   Jen Todd, "Music City Hot Air Balloon Festival," *Tennessean*, August 27, 2015. Available online: http://www.tennessean.com/story/life/family/2015/08/26/music-city-hot-air-balloon-festival-lights-warner-park/32352693/.

32   Phyllis Heard, interview transcript, Nashville, Tennessee, June 11, 2014, *West End Home Collection*, Metropolitan Nashville Archives.

33   Cemele Richardson, interview transcript, Nashville, Tennessee, June 11, 2014, *West End Home Collection*, Metropolitan Nashville Archives. Edith Miller was the mother of Cemele Richardson. "Italian Street Fair Party," *Tennessean*, August 14, 1980.

34   Jean Ward Oldfield, interview by author, Nashville, Tennessee, January 2017.

35   *Nashville Tennessean*, c. 1960, Scrapbook, *West End Home Collection*, Metropolitan Nashville Archives.

36   "Rag Catches Fire," *Tennessean*, November 27, 1961.

37   Charter of Incorporation, 1892, *West End Home Foundation Collection*, Metropolitan Nashville Archives.

38   Nettie Jane Langhans, interview with Drake Calton, Nashville, Tennessee, June 11, 2014, *West End Home Foundation Collection*, Metropolitan Nashville Archives.

39   Betty Sue Parrish McNeilly, interview transcript, Nashville, Tennessee, June 11, 2014, *West End Home Foundation Collection*, Metropolitan Nashville Archives.

40   Interview transcripts, Nashville, Tennessee, June 11, 2014, *West End Home Collection*, Metropolitan Nashville Archives.

41   Patricia Ingram Hart, interview by author, Brentwood, Tennessee, February 28, 2017.

42   "The West End Home for Ladies Notes to the Financial Statements for 1983," *West End Home Collection*, Metropolitan Nashville Archives. The appraisal value in 2016 for 2817 West End Avenue was 11.1 million dollars (7.9 million in land, and 3.2 million in structures).

43   Patricia Ingram Hart, interview by author, Brentwood, Tennessee, February 28, 2017.

44 Nettie Jane Langhans, interview with Drake Calton, Nashville, Tennessee, June 11, 2014, *West End Home Collection*, Metropolitan Nashville Archives.

45 Cindy Dickinson, interview by author, February 16, 2017. Drake Calton, interview transcript, Nashville, Tennessee, June 11, 2014, *West End Home Collection*, Metropolitan Nashville Archives.

46 Anne Coleman, interview with Grace Awh, Nashville, Tennessee, June 11, 2014, *West End Home Collection*, Metropolitan Nashville Archives.

47 Cindy Dickinson, interview by author, February 16, 2017.

48 Patricia Ingram Hart, interview by author, Brentwood, Tennessee, February 28, 2017.

49 Sarah McConnell, interview by author, Nashville, Tennessee, January 18, 2017.

50 Ibid.

51 Anne Coleman, interview with Grace Awh, Nashville, Tennessee, June 11, 2014, *West End Home Collection*, Metropolitan Nashville Archives.

52 Emmie McDonald, interview transcript, Nashville, Tennessee, June 11, 2014, *West End Home Collection*, Metropolitan Nashville Archives.

53 Gayle Vance, interview by author, Nashville, Tennessee, February 23, 2017.

54 Nettie Jane Langhans, interview with Drake Calton, Nashville, Tennessee, June 11, 2014, *West End Home Collection*, Metropolitan Nashville Archives.

55 Jean Ward Oldfield, interview transcription, Nashville, Tennessee, June 11, 2014, *West End Home Collection*, Metropolitan Nashville Archives.

56 Sarah McConnell, interview by author, Nashville, Tennessee, January 20, 2017.

57 Peggy Miller, interview by author, Nashville, Tennessee, January 17, 2017.

58 Grace Bathrick, interview with Drake Calton, Nashville, Tennessee, June 11, 2014, *West End Home Collection*, Metropolitan Nashville Archives.

59 Ibid.

60 Cindy Dickinson, interview by author, Nashville, Tennessee, February 6, 2017.

61 Jean Ward Oldfield, interview, Nashville, Tennessee, June 11, 2014, *West End Home Collection*, Metropolitan Nashville Archives.

62 *West End Home for Ladies Newsletter*, 2002, *West End Home Collection*, Metropolitan Nashville Archives.

63 Anne Coleman, interview with Grace Awh, Nashville, Tennessee, June 11, 2014, *West End Home Collection*, Metropolitan Nashville Archives.

64 Cindy Dickinson, interview by author, Nashville, Tennessee, February 6, 2017.

65 Financial Information for Josephine Sweeney, Jennie Mae Clark, Susan Brandau, *West*

End Home Collection, Metropolitan Nashville Archives.

66   Carole Nelson, interview by author, Nashville, Tennessee, January 17, 2017.

67   Ibid.

68   Gray Thornburg, interview by author, Nashville, Tennessee, February 28, 2017.

Chapter 4

1   Jean Ward Oldfield, interview with author, Nashville, Tennessee, January 16, 2017.

2   Gayle Vance, interview with author, Nashville, Tennessee, February 23, 2017.

3   Tom Delvaux, "Our Legacy of Caring," *West End Home Foundation*. Available online: https://www.westendhomefoundation.org/our-legacy-of-caring/.

4   William C. Thomas, Jr., *Nursing Homes and Public Policy: Drift and Decision in New York State* (Ithaca: Cornell University Press, 1969), 256.

5   Ibid., vii-ix.

6   Cindy Dickinson, interview with author, January 31, 2017, Available online: https://www.westendhomefoundation.org/our-legacy-of-caring/. The specific numbers of residents per decade are as follows: 1960–1969: 62; 1970–1979: 45; 1980–1989: 39; 1990–1999: 39; 2000–2012: 30.

7   Jean Farris, interview with author, Nashville, Tennessee, January 19, 2017.

8   Carole Haber, "Nursing Homes: History," Available online: http://medicine.jrank.org/pages/1243/Nursing-Homes-History.html.

9   "A Profile of Older Americans: 2015," *Department of Health and Human Services* (Washington, DC: Department of Health and Human Services, 2015), 3. Available online: https://aoa.acl.gov/aging_statistics/profile/2015/docs/2015-profile.pdf. The population of Americans over the age of sixty-five is projected to more than double to 98 million in 2060.

10   Cindy Dickinson, "Past Residents," *West End Home Foundation*. Available online: https://www.westendhomefoundation.org/our-legacy-of-caring/alumni/

11   "Kathryn Craig Henry," *Tennessean*, November 24, 1990.

12   Ibid.

13   "Ruth Rodemyer Weaver," *Tennessean*, March 29, 1994. Weaver's life of service began when she left Pine Manor College in Wellesley, Massachusetts, to work in Barnes Hospital (St. Louis, Missouri) during World War II. Membership in other civic and social organizations included the Daughter of the American Revolution, Centennial

Club, Belle Meade Country Club, and Colonial Dames of America.

14   Gayle Vance, interview with author, Nashville, Tennessee, February 23, 2017.

15   "Eight Killed in Fire at Nashville Nursing Home," *Associated Press*, September 26, 2003. Available online: http://www.foxnews.com/story/2003/09/26/eight-killed-in-fire-at-nashville-nursing-home.html.

16   Gayle Vance, interview with author, Nashville, Tennessee, February 23, 2017.

17   N. Courtney Hollins, interview with author, Nashville, Tennessee, February 22, 2017.

18   Gray Thornburg, interview with author, Nashville, Tennessee, February 28, 2017.

19   Jean Farris, interview with author, Nashville, Tennessee, January 19, 2017.

20   Gayle Vance, interview with author, Nashville, Tennessee, February 23, 2017.

21   Jean Farris, interview with author, Nashville, Tennessee, January 19, 2017.

22   Peggy Miller, interview with author, Nashville, Tennessee, January 20, 2017.

23   Gayle Vance, interview with author, Nashville, Tennessee, February 23, 2017.

24   Ibid.

25   Terronda Henderson, interview with author, February 21, 2017.

26   Peggy Miller, interview with author, Nashville, Tennessee, January 20, 2017.

27   Gayle Vance, interview with author, Nashville, Tennessee, February 23, 2017.

28   Peggy Miller, interview with author, Nashville, Tennessee, March 24, 2017.

29   Gayle Vance, interview with author, Nashville, Tennessee, February 23, 2017.

30   Ibid.

31   Ibid.; Gray Thornburg, interview with author, Nashville, Tennessee, February 28, 2017.

32   "Services at the Blakeford." Available online: http://blakeford.com/the-blakeford-family/services/

33   Ibid.

34   Gayle Vance, interview with author, Nashville, Tennessee, February 23, 2017.

35   Jean Farris, interview with author, Nashville, Tennessee, January 19, 2017.

36   Terronda Henderson, interview with author, February 21, 2017.

37   Jean Farris, interview with author, Nashville, Tennessee, January 19, 2017.

38   *West End Home for Ladies Handbook*, *West End Home Collection*, Metropolitan Archives of Nashville and Davidson County, 2008.

39   Gayle Vance, interview with author, Nashville, Tennessee, February 23, 2017.

40   Jean Ward Oldfield, interview with author, Nashville, Tennessee, January 16, 2017.

41   Jean Farris, interview with author, Nashville, Tennessee, January 19, 2017.

42   "Our Legacy of Caring," *West End Home Foundation* 2013. Available online: https://www.westendhomefoundation.org/our-legacy-of-caring/.

43   Gray Thornburg, speech transcript, *West End Home Foundation Collection*, Metropolitan Nashville Archives, June 11, 2014.

44   Marsha Edwards letter to West End Home Foundation, 2011, *West End Home Foundation Collection*, Metropolitan Nashville Archives.

45   "NPT Receives 2017 Grant From the West End Home Foundation," *Nashville Public Television*, November 7, 2016. Available online: http://blogs.wnpt.org/mediaupdate/2016/11/07/2017-west-end-home-foundation/.

46   Courtney Hollins, speech transcript, *West End Home Foundation Collection*, Metropolitan Nashville Archives, June 11, 2014.

47   Dianne Oliver, interview with author, Nashville, Tennessee, March 6, 2017.

48   Paul Arnsberger, Melissa Ludlum, Margaret Riley, and Mark Stanton, "A History of the Tax-Exempt Sector: An SOI Perspective," *Statistics of Income Bulletin* (Winter 2008) 121–22.

49   "Quick Facts About Nonprofits," *National Center for Charitable Giving Statistics* (NCCS). Available online: http://nccs.urban.org/data-statistics/quick-facts-about-nonprofits.

50   "Nonprofits Organizations in the United States," *Guidestar.* Available online: http://www.guidestar.org/rxg/analyze-nonprofit-data/nonprofits-in-the-united-states.aspx.

51   Paul Arnsberger, Melissa Ludlum, Margaret Riley, and Mark Stanton, "A History of the Tax-Exempt Sector: An SOI Perspective," *Statistics of Income Bulletin* (Winter 2008) 111–14.

52   "Statistics," *Giving USA*, 2015. Available online: http://www.givingusa.org.

53   Lester M. Salamon, ed., *The State of Non-Profit America* (Washington, DC.: Brookings Institute Press, 2002), 505.

54   Jean Farris, interview with author, Nashville, Tennessee, January 19, 2017.

55   Prior to her appointment, Oliver served as a consultant and trainer for the Center for Nonprofit Management in Nashville. She has a bachelor's degree in sociology from St. Olaf College in Northfield, Minnesota and a master's degree in sociology and gerontology from the University of Missouri-Kansas City.

56   Dianne Oliver, interview with author, Nashville, Tennessee, March 6, 2017.

57   Gray Thornburg, interview with author, February 28, 2017, Nashville, Tennessee.

58   Dianne Oliver, interview with author, Nashville, Tennessee, March 6, 2017.

59   Jean Ward Oldfield, interview with author, Nashville, Tennessee, January 16, 2017.

60   N. Courtney Hollins, interview with author, Nashville, Tennessee, February 22, 2017.

61   Gray Thornburg, interview with author, February 28, 2017, Nashville, Tennessee.

62   Excerpt from "East Coker" from FOUR QUARTETS by T.S. Eliot. Copyright ©
      1940 by T.S. Eliot. Copyright © renewed 1968 by Esme Valerie Eliot. Reprinted by
      permission of Houghton Mifflin Harcourt Publishing Company. All rights reserved.

Chapter 5

1   "Paul F. Tavel Papers, 1837–1900," Southern Historical Collection, The Wilson
     Library, University of North Carolina at Chapel Hill. Available online: http://
     finding-aids.lib.unc.edu/03017/.

2   "Acts of Tennessee, Chapter 131," *Tennessee State Library and Archives.* Available online:
     http://teva.contentdm.oclc.org/cdm/compoundobject/collection/p15138coll18/
     id/1997/rec/1.

3   Information obtained from death certificate as noted by Syd Gardner in 2016.
     Available online: http://bit.ly/2ouVrzC.

4   *The Daily American,* August 1, 1888, 4.

5   Thomas Hardy, *Tess of the d'Urbervilles* (New York: Harper & Brothers, 1893), 301.

6   *U.S. Census Records,* 1910; *Nashville City Directory,* 1910.

7   George Zepp, "West End Home for Ladies recalls the need of war widows," *Tennesseean,*
     August 21, 2002, 4.

8   Ibid.

9   "Cora Elizabeth Haley Green Fitzhugh," *West End Home Foundation,* available online:
     https://www.westendhomefoundation.org/cora-e-fitzhugh-2/.

10   "Letter to the Editor," *Tennessean,* April 10, 1949, 15.

11   "Lucy A. Foreman," *West End Home Foundation,* Available online: https://www.
     westendhomefoundation.org/lucy-foreman/.

12   Ibid.

13   "Susan Elsie Morrison Riley," *West End Home Foundation.* Available online: https://www.
     westendhomefoundation.org/susan-riley/.

14   Shapiro, John Lawton (1915–1983). Eskind Biomedical Library Special Collections,
     Vanderbilt University Medical Center, Nashville, Tennessee. Available online: https://
     www.library.vanderbilt.edu/biomedical/sc_diglib/archColl/870.html.

15   William Willard Howard, "The Rush to Oklahoma," *Harper's Weekly* 33 (May 18,
     1889), 391–94.

16   "Susan Elsie Morrison Riley," *West End Home Foundation.* Available online: https://www. westendhomefoundation.org/susan-riley/.

17   *American Baptist Yearbook,* (Philadelphia: The American Baptist Publishing Society), 1917. Available online: http://bit.ly/2oFqE5K.

18   "Celebrating 125 Years," *Tennessee Baptist Children's Home.* Available online: http:// tennesseechildren.org/about/.

19   "Susan Elsie Morrison Riley," *West End Home Foundation.* Available online: https://www. westendhomefoundation.org/susan-riley/.

20   "Ellen Jane Douglas Jones Ginn," *West End Home Foundation.* Available online: https:// www.westendhomefoundation.org/ellen-ginn/.

21   Women's Missionary Union. Available online: http://www.wmu.com/?q=article/ national-wmu/missions-discipleship-through-wmu.

22   "Ellen Jane Douglas Jones Ginn," *West End Home Foundation.* Available online: https://www. westendhomefoundation.org/ellen-ginn/.

23   Douglas Jones Ginn, *As I Saw It: Seventy-Year History of the Tennessee Women's Missionary Union* (Nashville: Women's Missionary Union, Auxiliary to the Tennessee Baptist Convention), 1958.

24   Women's Missionary Union. Available online: http://www.wmu.com/?q=article/ national-wmu/missions-discipleship-through-wmu.

25   "Ellen Jane Douglas Jones Ginn," *West End Home Foundation.* Available online: https:// www.westendhomefoundation.org/ellen-ginn/.

26   "History," *Metropolitan Development and Housing Agency* (2015). Available online: http:// www.nashville-mdha.org/history/.

27   Susan Brandau, "Cayce Retired? Not On Your Life!" *Tennessean,* Nov. 17, 1974.

28   Ibid.

29   Ibid.

30   Cindy Dickinson, interview with author, Nashville, Tennessee, December 10, 2016. Available online: https://www.westendhomefoundation.org/mary-cayce/.

31   Philip Sydney, quoted in *Civilization's Quotation: Life's Ideal,* Richard Alan Krieger (ed.), (New York: Algora Publishing), 308.

32   "Mary McCullough Keith," *West End Home Foundation.* Available online: https://www. westendhomefoundation.org/mary-keith/.

33   Ibid.

34   Ibid.

35   Janie Macey, interview with Grace Awh, Nashville Tennessee, June 11, 2014.

36   "Mary McCullough Keith," *West End Home Foundation*. Available online: https://www.
      westendhomefoundation.org/mary-keith/.

37   Jean Ward Oldfield, interview with author, Nashville, Tennessee, January 2017.

38   *Automobile Topics* 48, no. 1 (November 24 1917), 271. Available online: http://bit.
      ly/2mS9ygQ; "O. Armleder & Co. 1876–1922, Cincinnati, Ohio," *Encyclopedia of
      American Coachbuilders and Coachbuilding*, 2017. Available online: http://www.coachbuilt.
      com/bui/a/armleder/armleder.htm.

39   Cindy Dickinson, interview with author, Nashville, Tennessee, March 20, 2017.

40   Ibid.

41   "Eleanor Hersh," *West End Home Foundation*, 2007. Available online: https://www.
      westendhomefoundation.org/eleanor-hersch/.

42   *West End Home For Ladies Newsletter*, May 2000, *West End Home Foundation Collection*,
      Metropolitan Nashville Archives."

43   Jane Langhans, interview with Drake Calton, Nashville, Tennessee, June 11, 2014.

44   "Eleanor Hersh," *West End Home Foundation*, 2007. Available online: https://www.
      westendhomefoundation.org/eleanor-hersch/.

45   Peggy Miller, interview with author, Nashville, Tennessee, January 17, 2017.

46   Ibid.

Selected Bibliography

Archival Primary Sources:

West End Home Foundation Collection, Metropolitan Nashville Archives

Additional Archival Collections:

Act of Tennessee Collection, Tennessee State Library and Archives

John Shapiro Collection, Eskind Biomedical Library Special Collection, Vanderbilt University

Southern Historical Collection, The Wilson Library, University of North Carolina at Chapel Hill

Quaker Collection, Haverford College Library Special Collections, Haverford College

Periodicals:

American Baptist Yearbook

Annual Report of State Superintendent for Tennessee

Associated Press

Automobile Topics

Harper's Weekly

Journal of Economic Perspectives

Nashville Banner

Nashville City Directory

Nashville Daily American

Nashville Tennessean

Social Security Bulletin

Southwestern Reporter

Tennessean

Who's Who in Tennessee

Interviews:

Cindy Dickinson

Jean Dobson Farris

Jay Grannis

Patricia Ingram Hart

Terronda Henderson

N. Courtney Hollins

Sarah McConnell

Peggy Miller

Carol Minton Nelson

Jean Ward Oldfield

Dianne Oliver

Gray Oliver Thornburg

Gayle Deerborn Vance

Ridley Wills II

Additional Sources:

"A Profile of Older Americans: 2015." *Department of Health and Human Services.* Washington, DC: Department of Health and Human Services, 2015. https://aoa.acl.gov/aging_ statistics/profile/2015/docs/2015-profile.pdf.

Altman, Nancy J. *The Battle for Social Security: From FDR's Vision to Bush's Gamble.* Hoboken, NJ: John Wiley & Sons, 2005.

Arnsberger, Paul, Melissa Ludlum, Margaret Riley, and Mark Stanton, "A History of the Tax-Exempt Sector: An SOI Perspective," *Statistics of Income Bulletin* (Winter 2008): 105-135.

Bergeron, Paul, Stephen V. Ash, and Jeanette Keith. *Tennesseans and Their History.* Knoxville: University of Tennessee Press, 1999.

Clayton, W. Woodford. *History of Davidson County, Tennessee, with Illustrations and Biographical Sketches of its Prominent Men and Pioneers*. Philadelphia: J. W. Lewis & Co., 1880.

Delvaux, Tom. "Our Legacy of Caring." *West End Home Foundation*. https://www.westendhomefoundation.org/our-legacy-of-caring/.

Dickinson, Cindy. "Past Residents," *West End Home Foundation*. https://www.westendhomefoundation.org/our-legacy-of-caring/alumni/

Doyle, Don. *Nashville in the New South, 1880–1930*. Knoxville: University of Tennessee Press, 1985.

Eliot, T.S. "East Coker" from FOUR QUARTETS. Copyright © 1940 by T.S. Eliot. Copyright © renewed 1968 by Esme Valerie Eliot. Excerpt reprinted by permission of Houghton Mifflin Harcourt Publishing Company. All rights reserved.

Haber, Carole. "Nursing Homes: History." http://medicine.jrank.org/pages/1243/Nursing-Homes-History.html.

Haber, Carole and Brian Gratton. *Old Age and the Search for Security*. New York: Cambridge University Press, 1994.

Hall, Peter Dobkin. *Inventing the Nonprofit Sector and Other Essays on Philanthropy, Voluntarism, and Nonprofit Organizations*. Baltimore: John Hopkins Press, 1992.

Howard, Memucan Hunt. *Recollections of Tennessee*. Nashville: Tennessee Historical Society, 1883. http://www.tnyesterday.com/yesterday_henderson/recolltn.html.

"James C. McReynolds." *Oyez*. Chicago: Chicago-Kent College of Law at Illinois Tech. https://www.oyez.org/justices/james_c_mcreynolds.

McSteen, Martha. "Fifty Years of Social Security." *Social Security Bulletin* 48 (August 1985): 38–50.

"Nonprofits Organizations in the United States." *Guidestar*. http://www.guidestar.org/rxg/analyze-nonprofit-data/nonprofits-in-the-united-states.aspx.

"NPT Receives 2017 Grant From the West End Home Foundation." *Nashville Public Television*, November 7, 2016. http://blogs.wnpt.org/mediaupdate/2016/11/07/2017-west-end-home-foundation/.

"Quick Facts About Nonprofits," *National Center for Charitable Giving Statistics* (NCCS). http://nccs.urban.org/data-statistics/quick-facts-about-nonprofits.

Roosevelt, Eleanor. "My Day, October 6, 1938." *The Eleanor Roosevelt Papers Digital Edition*. Washington D.C.: George Washington University, 2008. https://www2.gwu.edu/~erpapers/myday/displaydoc.cfm?_y=1938&_f=md055077.

Rowles, Graham D., and Pamela B. Teaster. *Long-Term Care in an Aging Society: Theory and Practice*. New York: Spring Publishing, 2016.

Salamon, Lester M., ed. *The State of Non-Profit America*. Washington, DC.: Brookings Institute Press, 2002.

Slatery, Herbert H. *Tennessee's New Non-Profit Corporation Act: A Flexible and Modern Statutory Approach*. Nashville: M. Lee Smith, 1987.

Soodalter, Ron. "William Walker: King of the 19th Century Filibuster." March 4, 2010, http://www.historynet.com/.

Spinney, Robert Guy. *World War II in Nashville: Transformation of the Homefront*. Knoxville: University of Tennessee Press, 1998.

"The Roosevelts Visit Nashville." *Nashville Public Library Off the Shelf Series*. November 2014, http://nashvillepubliclibrary.org.

"The Social Security Act of 1935." *Social Security Administration*. https://www.ssa.gov/history/35act.html.

Thomas Jr., William C. *Nursing Homes and Public Policy: Drift and Decision in New York State*. Ithaca: Cornell University Press, 1969.

"Will Allen Dromgoole (1860–1934)." *The Poetry Foundation*, 2017. https://www.poetryfoundation.org/poems-and-poets/poets/detail/will-allen-dromgoole.